Steve Caplin is a photomontage expert and the author of several bestselling books on computer graphics. He's passionate about technology, and likes nothing more than tinkering with the latest gadgets, software and power tools. He divides his spare time between playing the accordion and repairing his children's iPods.

Simon Rose is a film critic, award-winning screenwriter and author. He likes country walks and playing cricket, and loves trying out new games with his children. Simon plays the cello and the spoons. He's the proud owner of a shiny new MP3 player, and looks forward to hours of happy listening once Steve shows him how to use it.

D1510767

By the same authors:
Dad Stuff
More Dad Stuff
Stuff the Turkey
Complete and Utter Zebu

By Steve Caplin:
How to Cheat in Photoshop (6 editions)
Art & Design in Photoshop
100% Photoshop
How to Cheat in Photoshop Elements (4 editions, with David Asch)
Max Pixel's Adventures in Adobe Photoshop Elements
The Complete Guide to Digital Illustration (with Adam Banks)
Icon Design

By Simon Rose:
Classic Film Guide
Radio 1 FM Essential Film Guide
Collins Gem Classic Film Guide
The Book of Brilliant Hoaxes
Tips From a Top Tycoon (with Gail Renard)
Filthy Lucre
The Shareholder: The Truth about Wider Share Ownership
Fair Shares: A Beginner's Guide to the Stock Market

FUN AND GAMES
FOR THE 21ST CENTURY FAMILY

Steve Caplin & Simon Rose

Acknowledgments

Thanks to Tobin and Jenna Chapman and all the Gallimores
for agreeing to appear in our photographs.
Thanks to Joseph, Connie and Izzy Rose, and Freddy and Joe Caplin,
for being willing guinea pigs.
Special thanks to BYB for services above and beyond the call of publishing.

First published in 2010 by Old Street Publishing Ltd
Yowlestone House, Puddington, Tiverton, Devon EX16 8LN
www.oldstreetpublishing.co.uk

ISBN 978-1-906964-43-6

The authors have taken every care to ensure that the facts they present in this book are
accurate at the time of going to press. In the event that any party wishes to challenge
the information contained herein, the authors will be happy to hear from them. All such
communications should be directed via the publisher.

10 9 8 7 6 5 4 3 2 1

A CIP catalogue record for this title is available from the British Library.

Designed and typeset by Steve Caplin.
Printed and bound in Great Britain by CPI Mackays, Chatham ME5 8TD

Contents

Fun

The 6-step film course

Appendix

Steve Caplin

Simon Rose

Introduction

Some pundits complain that technology is the enemy of family life. We think they're wrong. We believe the gadgets in our homes can bring families together to have fun – real old-fashioned, laugh-out-loud family fun.

This book is stuffed with over 200 games and activities, many using the technology you already own – not just digital cameras and mobile phones, but also everyday appliances such as toasters and even hair-dryers. Most have a modern twist, but you don't need to be a technical whizz to enjoy them.

You'll need to muster all your ingenuity and imagination to become everything from a spy master to a security camera, from a space invader to a Sat Nav. And because we know some games will never become obsolete, we've included a selection of tried-and-tested classics.

On each page in this book, icons show the suggested age range, number of players, type of game, and equipment needed.

The **Games** section comprises activities with a clearly defined structure and set of rules, often ending with a winner. The **Fun** section covers a range of more open-ended pastimes, such as trick photography or stop-motion animation, that we hope will get your creative juices flowing. In the **6-Step Film Course** we give some tips on how to get the most from your video camera to make films your audience will actually want to watch, and the **Appendix** provides clear instructions for some of the more techy stuff.

If you're looking for a game or activity for a specific occasion, head for the **Index**, where all the activities are listed by type, so you can find the perfect entertainment in an instant. And if you come up with your own variations, use the **Notes** section to jot them down – and please do share them with us and other readers through our website at *www.fg-21.com*.

We talk about a 'Fun and Games revolution', which may seem over the top. But we really do believe a whole new universe of family fun and creativity is out there, just waiting to be explored.

Steve Caplin & Simon Rose
London, 2010

GAM

game *(n.)*: a form of play or sport, esp. a competitive one played according to rules and decided by skill, strength, or luck.

All ages

2+
Players

Indoor

Stopwatch/timer

Alphabet countdown

Use a countdown timer with sound effects to add extra tension and hilarity to these classic alphabet games.

SET UP 1 min | **PLAY TIME 5+ mins** | **YOU NEED** a mobile phone with a timer function

All mobile phones are equipped with timers, which can be a boon if you've lost the egg-timer from an old board game. But electronic timers can also spice up a whole range of games – and with an alarm sound that plays when time is up, they're far more dramatic than just waiting for the last grains of sand to trickle through.

Animal alphabet

In this game, players must name animals starting with consecutive letters of the alphabet. 'Ant' might be followed by 'baboon', then 'cougar' and so on up to 'Z' and then back to 'A' again, leaving out only 'X'.

Each player has three lives. The person in charge of the game sets the phone timer for anything up to a couple of minutes, then places the phone face down on the table. With the display hidden, none of the players can see how long the timer has to run.

The first player rests their hand on the the phone. As soon as they've thought of an animal starting with 'A', they say it aloud then slide the timer to the next player, who puts their hand on it until they've thought of a 'B', and then slides it to the next player, and so on. The phone becomes a ticking bomb, to be got rid of as quickly as possible. If the alarm goes off while you're still thinking, you lose a life.

You can also play this game with countries, cities, foods, names or household objects – or in fact just about anything.

TIP: *Make the game instantly more difficult with a simple extra twist – use the alphabet backwards.*

Change the subject

In this variation, the topic changes with each move. So if one player has to name an animal, they might say 'hippopotamus', then choose the subject for the next player e.g. 'a country'. The next player might then say 'India', and change the topic to, for example, 'a flower', leaving the player after them to say 'jasmine' and so on.

Alphabet sentence

For a bigger challenge, players have to construct sentences using words beginning with consecutive letters. A typical sentence might go: 'A... busy... copper... directed... eight... fire-engines... going... home...' and so on.

When the alarm goes off, the player caught with the phone must repeat the entire mad sentence, getting all the words right. If they make any mistakes, they lose one of their lives.

GOING FURTHER

Many phones let you choose the noise that goes off when a timer finishes. Make it an explosion, or a crazy laugh or a duck, for example. Younger kids in particular love this.

3

Indoor

Brain power

Bike lock codebreaker

Summon all your powers of logic and strategy to break the secret code and guess the four-digit combination.

SET UP 10 mins | **PLAY TIME 15+ mins** | **YOU NEED** a combination cycle lock or padlock

The commercial game *Mastermind*, invented in 1970, is a variation of an older code-breaking game called Bulls & Cows, which was based around numbers rather than coloured pegs.

Our version uses a bicycle combination lock (or any other type of combination lock), which is not only more tactile than plastic pegs but also adds a couple of interesting twists.

The original *Mastermind* game had pegs of six different colours while combination locks use ten numbers, so we've tweaked the game a little to simplify it. But there's no reason why you can't make it more difficult when playing with more experienced code-breakers.

Setting up

You need not only a four-digit lock, but also the know-how to change the combination. The chances are that the instructions have long since been mislaid. It shouldn't matter.

With most cycle locks, you dial in the current code, open the lock and then flip a lever or turn a wheel. This allows you to alter the combination, which is then fixed by returning the lever or wheel to its original position. For obvious reasons, write the new number down before you spin the dials to conceal the combination, or you may find yourself playing this game for much longer than you expected.

To prepare the game, the code-maker sets four numbers as the new combination, being sure to use each number only once – otherwise the game gets a whole lot trickier.

How to play

Once the code-maker has set the new combination, the lock is handed to the code-breaker, who dials four random numbers. After trying to pull the lock open (after all, they might strike it lucky on the first attempt), the code-breaker hands the lock back. The code-maker tells them: (a) which numbers are correct and in the right position; (b) which numbers are correct but in the wrong position. So the code-maker might say: 'Number 2 is correct and in the right position, and number 4 is correct but in the wrong position.'

In the original *Mastermind*, the code-breaker wasn't told which entries were correct or incorrect, just the number of correct guesses. But with ten digits to juggle, our change seems sensible.

The code-breaker leaves any numbers in the correct position alone, tries numbers that are in the wrong position in a different location, and dials new numbers elsewhere. And so the game continues, until the code-breaker is able to open the lock.

Code-breaking strategies

There should be no need for the code-breaker to write anything down: it's fairly easy to remember which numbers are correct and in the right position, which need to be moved to another position, and which haven't yet been tried. Beginners could try starting with '1234' as their first guess: that way it's even easier to keep track.

GOING FURTHER

For a more difficult game, have the code-maker only say how many digits are correct, not which ones. It's much harder this way, and the code-breaker will need a pen and paper to write down their attempted combinations.

There are, of course, five-digit locks which have 100,000 possible combinations, rather than the paltry 10,000 on a four-digit lock.

Camera quickdraw

Defend your honour by challenging your opponent to a duel – using camera phones instead of pistols.

SET UP **2 mins** | PLAY TIME **3+ mins** | YOU NEED two phones with cameras

It's a familiar scene to anyone fond of old movies. Two duellists stand back-to-back, their weapons at the ready. At a given signal, the combatants take ten paces, turn and fire.

Using phones equipped with cameras instead of pistols, you can recreate the tension and excitement of duelling with less fatal results. Players must 'hit' their opponent by taking a photo of them – but must avoid being 'hit' in return.

Setting up

As in a traditional duel, the players agree the number of paces to be taken. For the sake of realism, try to avoid crashing into the furniture or getting tangled in a hedge. If your playing area is a small one, take short heel-to-toe paces rather than long strides.

You must also decide whether to start with the phones already 'loaded' or not ('loaded' meaning that they are already switched to camera mode). Our preference is for the phones to be in standby mode: fumbling desperately to turn the camera on is part of the fun.

How to play

The players stand back-to-back, phones held at their sides with fingers off the buttons. If two other people are around they can act as 'seconds', ensuring there is no foul play. Starting at the same time, the two players then take the agreed number of paces, counting aloud so they remain in sync. They then spin round and, one-handed, put the phone into camera mode and try to snap a photo of the other player as quickly as possible. Only one 'shot' is allowed.

As soon as a player has 'fired' once, they should spin round and crouch or sit down on the ground, with their back to their opponent.

How to score

When both players have taken their photos, the phones are compared. Award ten points for a deadly shot – a picture in which the front or the side of the opponent's entire head and torso has been caught in the frame. A picture showing some but not all of the head and torso, or other body parts, scores five points. There are no points for a picture of the *back* of the head or body: for the purposes of the game we must imagine the players are wearing tortoise-like protective shells.

Since the cameras on some phones are easier to use than others, it helps make the game fairer to play it twice, with phones swapped over between rounds.

GOING FURTHER

Try playing the game with both players blindfolded (see page 223 for how to make a blindfold). The more paces that are taken, the more chance there is of capturing an image of your opponent.

Or instead of having phones held by their sides, consider starting with the phones nestling in the duellists' pockets, making the drawing of their weapons that bit more difficult.

Age 5+

2+

Players

Car game

Car bingo

Keep kids entertained on car journeys – and encourage them to look out of the window at the same time.

SET UP 10 mins | PLAY TIME 30+ mins | YOU NEED a computer to print the bingo sheets

The trouble with car journeys is not just that kids get bored, it's that they spend so much time plugged into media players and portable games consoles that they barely glance out of the window. Here's a selection of games to get them looking out at their surroundings.

Town and country bingo

Players must spot the 20 objects on the sheet, ticking them off as they do so. We've provided two versions, for both town and country roads:

fg-21.com/carbingo.pdf

We've also provided a couple of blank cards, so you can fill in your own items to be spotted.

Fun and Games for the 21st Century Family

Car Bingo

Sheet 1: Country roads

☐ Post box	☐ Tractor
☐ Sheep	☐ Pig
☐ Cow	☐ Village sign
☐ Level crossing	☐ Dustbin
☐ Haystack	☐ Dead tree
☐ Horse	☐ Cat
☐ Pub	☐ Pond
☐ Phone box	☐ Water tower
☐ Thatched house	☐ Electricity pylon
☐ Church	☐ Bicycle

Tick each box as you spot the object

Fun and Games for the 21st Century Family

Car Bingo

Sheet 2: Town roads

☐ Pub	☐ Hotel
☐ Train station	☐ Traffic warden
☐ Ambulance	☐ Hairdresser
☐ Policeman	☐ Roadworks
☐ Fire station	☐ Cat
☐ Taxi	☐ Speed camera
☐ Zebra crossing	☐ Learner driver
☐ Supermarket	☐ White van
☐ Estate agent	☐ Indian takeaway
☐ Butcher	☐ Car saleroom

Tick each box as you spot the object

Motorway driving

It's harder to come up with things to spot on motorways, since the scene is somewhat dominated by other cars. So make a game out of it.

Each player picks a car manufacturer – Ford, Toyota, Peugeot, etc. They then have to spot as many instances of that make as they can, scoring a point for each qualifying car they see.

Advanced scoring

If just spotting cars is too straightforward for you, try this variation. Rather than simply counting your chosen make of car, score one point for each one going in the opposite direction on the other side of the motorway, two points for each one you overtake, and three points for each one that passes you.

Each player can also pick a 'bonus' type of vehicle – a car transporter, a police car, an ambulance, a Marks & Spencer lorry, and so on. They score an additional ten points for any of these they spot.

Motorway variations

For younger players, who may have trouble recognising particular makes of car, play using colours rather than makes – though they won't take long to learn that silver is the most popular car colour.

Car-obsessed older players can play a version where they have to select not just a make, but a model as well – such as a Ford Galaxy, a Porsche 911, or a Jaguar S Type.

A practical extra

The first player to spot each speed camera gets 20 bonus points. It's worth it to save the driver three points of a rather less welcome sort on their licence.

GOING FURTHER

If you're driving on holiday in a foreign country, try getting the kids to spot all the GB stickers on the backs of cars – and give them extra points for working out the countries that other stickers belong to.

Celebrity spotter

2+

Players

Indoor

Computer

Race to guess the celebrity as their face is revealed spot by spot in this family quiz game.

| SET UP 20 mins | PLAY TIME 15+ mins | YOU NEED computer with internet • photos |

In this quiz game with a difference, it's up to the Quizmaster to decide which questions they want to ask: they could be anything from obscure dates or world capitals to questions about the family or the home.

On the screen is a photo of one of the contestants, with a celebrity hidden beneath it. Every time the players get a correct answer, the Quizmaster reveals a little more of the celebrity. The winner is the first to guess the identity of the hidden superstar.

Setting up

You need a picture of a celebrity (the cybersphere is awash with them) and another of a member of your family, both shot from the same angle. Open Pixlr (*www.pixlr.com* – see page 230 for how to use it).

Now open both pictures – you can type in the web address of the celebrity photo to load it. They will appear in separate windows within Pixlr.

Combine the images

With the photo of your family member 'live', choose Edit > Select All and then Edit > Copy. Close this window, and in the celebrity window, choose Edit > Paste. The photo will appear as a separate layer above the celebrity image. In the Layers panel, set the opacity of the pasted layer to 50%.

The celebrity image should be visible below the new layer. Choose Edit > Free Transform, and resize the image of your family member so their eyes and mouth align with the celebrity's. Set the opacity back to 100%.

How to play

Close the Layers panel window to hide the thumbnail image of the celebrity.

Now select the Eraser tool and choose a large, hard brush – 100 pixels or more. Assemble your panellists and begin asking them questions. With each correct answer use the Eraser to remove a bit more of the top image. If you want to make the contestants sweat, leave the eyes till last, as these are the most easily identifiable feature.

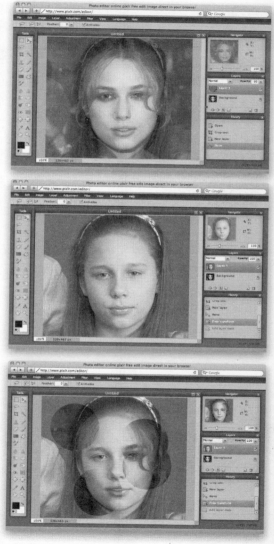

TIP: *For a version that's quicker to set up, use a plain colour instead of a family member as the top layer – then hide what- or whoever you like underneath.*

Churchill's war

Each family member gets to display their own area of expertise, but who's the best all-rounder?

SET UP 5 mins | **PLAY TIME 20+ mins** | **YOU NEED** a computer with internet access

This game tests players' knowledge of the lives of the famous. But with contestants taking it in turns to choose the subject, you may find you need to know as much about Lady Gaga as Lady Thatcher.

Setting Up

Players sit around a table or a room, with one player – the 'Quizmaster' – having control of the computer.

How to play

The Quizmaster picks a well-known historical, contemporary or fictional character about whom they think they know more than the other players. We'll take Winston Churchill as an example. They then type the name, in inverted commas, into the Google search field, as shown:

> "Winston Churchill"
>
> Google Search   I'm Feeling Lucky

Starting with the player to the Quizmaster's left, each other player then declares the single noun (say, 'war') that they believe will produce the most hits when entered into a Google search together with the famous person. As they do so, the Quizmaster types their suggested word into the search field after "Winston Churchill" and presses Search, as below:

Google | "winston churchill" war | Search
About 2,810,000 results (0.12 seconds) | Advanced search

The Quizmaster then writes down the number of hits returned, in this case 2,810,000. Obviously, players cannot pick a word already chosen by another player.

After all the other players have made their choice, the Quizmaster reads out all the results, from lowest to highest. The Quizmaster then has one chance to beat the top score with his or her own chosen word.

Moving on

After the Quizmaster's turn, another player takes the computer and becomes the Quizmaster, picking a new celebrity. Adults may feel pretty smug about getting a high score for Churchill, but how will they fare against their teenagers with 'Lady Gaga'? And will they flounder when younger children suggest 'Mr Tumble' or 'Tinky Winky'?

How to score

Each player simply scores the number of hits their word produced, with all the individual round's scores added up at the end. One of the satisfying things about this game is that even the loser's score is likely to run to many millions.

Variations

Try playing the same game, but this time players have to choose a second *person* to go with the first (you'll need to put quotation marks around them too). You could also try with the famous person plus a place, a colour, a types of fruit, a rodent, or (you probably get the idea) just about anything at all.

GOING FURTHER

As an alternative, try picking just a single word and seeing who can come up with the most number of hits. We found that 'BBC' produced 147 million hits, whereas 'Obama' turned up 180 million: and even he was beaten by 'God', with over 420 million hits. Can you find any that beat 'God'?

Continuity error

Test your audience's memory and alertness by making a film riddled with continuity errors.

| SET UP 1+ hr | PLAY TIME 20+ mins | YOU NEED a video camera and props |

Every feature film and television drama employs a Continuity Supervisor. Their job is to make careful notes on what each character is wearing, which buttons on their clothing are undone, how their hair is arranged, where blood and bruises have been painted on their faces, where props have been left in the scene, and so on.

It's a taxing job, but a necessary one: because scenes that are next to each other in the final movie may not be filmed on the same day – they could even be weeks apart – someone has to ensure that when a character enters a room, he or she is wearing the same clothes as they were seen in when opening the door from the other side.

Our game involves breaking as many of those rules as we can get away with.

Setting up

You need a reasonable cast of characters, a fairly 'busy' background, some changes of clothing, and a good selection of props.

The idea is to shoot scenes in order, one at a time, but making a single 'continuity error' change before each new shot. This means working out what you're going to do before you start filming, so you have plenty of props and clothes to hand. Your film can either be an ordinary home movie showing a slice of everyday family life, or you could try something more complicated with a plot and fictional characters.

These are the sort of changes you might make between each shot:

● Change one item of clothing

● Move a piece of furniture in the background – a chair or a cushion

- Give an actor in the background a book to read, and change it between scenes.

- Have an actor exit through one door, then film them reappearing through a different one

- Leave the curtains open in one shot, and close them in the next

- If one of your actors wears glasses, have them take them off between scenes

- Change the way an actor's hair is arranged

- Have a glass of orange juice (easier to see than water) on the table, with the level of juice going up and down between shots.

If you have two actors who look vaguely similar – or even if they don't – then a good trick is to get them to exchange clothes and swap positions between scenes. It's surprising how many people will completely fail to notice the change, particularly if they aren't the main focus of the scene.

It isn't compulsory to change just one thing per shot, of course, although it will be much harder for the audience to spot a whole load of changes in one go.

When the movie's finished

After you've shot all the scenes, edit them together if you need to – although you may find that no editing is necessary, especially if you want it to look like a regular home movie.

Now you're ready to show the finished film to another family or a group of friends. Give them points for each continuity error they manage to spot – and then you can have fun pointing out all the ones they missed.

GOING FURTHER

If you're looking for inspiration, try visiting the movie website **www.imdb.com**, which has a 'goofs' section in every film's entry.

Made a fantastic Continuity Error movie? Share it with the world!

fg-21.com/forum

Age 8+

2
Players

Indoor

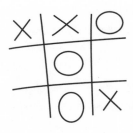

Remote friends

Dabbleboard: remote gaming

Creative and collaborative online drawing games for rainy days at home.

| SET UP 2 mins | PLAY TIME 10+ mins | YOU NEED two computers with internet access |

We've all played games that involve drawing. But we're used to being in the same room, using the same piece of paper as the other players. In the brave new cyber world, that doesn't have to be the case. You no longer even need paper. There are some excellent collaborative drawing websites that are fun in themselves, but which also lend themselves to games. These are great for playing with friends, but also ideal if, for instance, a parent is away on a business trip and still wants to be able to play with their child.

Our current favourite is Dabbleboard (www.dabbleboard.com). We explain how to use it on page 214. When you're linked with another person, whatever you draw on your screen appears on theirs too, in real time. What's more, you can be simultaneously linked by audio and video, Skype style, so that you can chat as you play. (Naturally, you can also play all these games just as happily face-to-face.)

Noughts and crosses

Also known as tic-tac-toe, this simplest of games is an excellent way of getting used to Dabbleboard.

Draw a grid, with 'freehand' mode turned off, then simply take it in turns to start, drawing noughts and crosses into the grid in the usual way.

Those with a penchant for orderliness may wish to create a store-house of perfect noughts and crosses in advance of the commencement of play. If you do like things neat, type out an 'X', highlight it and

16

change it to the largest font, then duplicate it as many times as you want by selecting it and clicking the icon at the top right. Noughts can be cloned in the same way; note that if you're after perfect circles or ovals, you should draw them with freehand mode turned off.

   During the actual game, the 'noughts and crosses you prepared earlier' can be dragged into position on the grid by highlighting them and using the icon at the top left corner.

Hangman

One player thinks of a word, then draws as many dashes as there are letters in the word. The other player guesses what letters might be in the word,

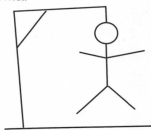

either by typing in the chat box, or by saying them out loud if the players are linked. Correctly guessed letters are written into the word; incorrect ones are written below and a piece of the gibbet is built.

   At the first wrong guess, draw in the base, then the vertical support, than a diagonal support at the top corner and finally the rope. Then the person is drawn: first their head, then their body and then their arms and legs. If the drawing is completed, the guesser has lost.

   Using Dabbleboard, it's neatest to draw one dash with freehand mode off, duplicate it several times and drag the dashes apart. The gibbet will look best if freehand mode is off. The body can be drawn just as easily in either mode.

   Use a large font size to type in the letters onto the empty dashes as they are guessed, making sure you keep a record somewhere on the screen of the wrongly guessed letters.

   The shorter the word, the harder it usually is to guess. Among our favourite hangman words are lynx, jinx, rhythm and ply.

GOING FURTHER

Noughts and Crosses can also be played a 'blind' game. Each player simply says where they are placing their symbol, without drawing it out, but using their mind's eye. It's a lot easier than blindfold chess, but still a challenge — and no doubt good for the grey cells.

Egg and toothbrush race

The egg and spoon race with a difference – no egg, no spoon, and an electric toothbrush adds vibration.

| SET UP 20 mins | PLAY TIME 15+ mins | YOU NEED electric toothbrush • yoghurt pot lid |

Although we remember them fondly from our childhoods, egg and spoon races seem so very 'last century' that it is hard to imagine today's children being keen to participate.

Not so our updated version, which uses an electric toothbrush instead of a spoon and doesn't need any eggs, either soft or hard-boiled, substituting coins instead.

Setting up

Take the brush head off the toothbrush, and find a plastic lid of the sort that comes with dips or larger yoghurts. Remove the last vestiges of taramasalata or yoghurt, and pierce the centre of the lid with a pair of scissors, making sure to keep the hole very small or the lid may split.

Ensure the electric toothbrush is fully charged. You need the main handle section with the motor, minus any attachments. With the lid facing downwards, force it over the bare metal end of the toothbrush and push down as far as it will go. Fasten it in place in a roughly horizontal position. A couple of pieces of sellotape should be enough to attach the lid to the toothbrush stem and stop it tipping too much to one side.

How to play

Set up a course for the players, which can be relatively straightforward or involve some obstacles to clamber over. Whether you play this inside or out, the obstacles should be soft in case of tumbles.

Each player places a two pence piece on the attached lid and turns on the toothbrush. With the lid vibrating thousands of times a minute, the player must manoeuvre the course as quickly as possible. If they drop the coin, they have to start all over again. To make things more difficult, a lighter coin such as penny can be used instead.

   If you're having a party and can get hold of an extra electric toothbrush, arrange for a relay race with two competing teams. Line up the players at alternate ends of the course and away you go.

TIP: *If it proves impossible to complete the course without dropping the coin, give a point for each drop. The player with the fewest points wins.*

GOING FURTHER

For a more fiendish challenge, try the race with a ping pong ball instead of the coin.

Tape: add tape both above and below the lid for a secure fix

Yoghurt lid: be sure to clean any old yoghurt off first or the coin will stick

Toothbrush: you'll need to remove the head, leaving just the spike

All ages

2+
Players

Indoor/Outdoor

Construction

Active

Mobile phone

Eye, Robot

Experience the world like a robot using our pioneering Robot Cereal Box Vision System™.

| SET UP 10 mins | PLAY TIME 20+ mins | YOU NEED an empty cereal box • a camera phone |

Mobile phone cameras are improving all the time, but they're still vastly inferior to our own eyes. It isn't only that they're less clear but, if the lens moves quickly, the image does not update instantly.

Using large cereal boxes and some sticky tape, we've found a way to turn camera phones into semi-blindfolds to impair players' vision for a range of games. See page 222 for how to construct our Robot Cereal Box Vision System (RCBVS). It only takes a couple of minutes to knock one up, and they're great fun.

Partially sighted person's buff

In traditional blind man's buff, somebody is blindfolded and they must try to catch other players, who try to keep out of their reach. Our high-tech version, with the seeker holding a cereal box to their head and viewing the field of play through a phone camera lens, is still surprisingly challenging – and certainly much funnier.

As a variant, if you're playing with eight or more people, have a pair of seekers with cereal boxes on their heads.

Robot obstacle course

For someone wearing the RCBVS, it's impossible to see straight ahead and keep an eye on the ground at the same time, making even normal walking pace hard to maintain. So why not make life really difficult and set up an obstacle course? It's a good idea to use soft objects such as cushions or coats in case of a robo-tumble. Either have one robot navigate the course at a time and record how long it takes them, or, if you have two RCBVS-equipped players, turn it into a race.

TECHNICAL NOTE

The camera phone we used switched itself to standby mode after a minute. Not all phones do this and it takes only one press of a button to start it again. However, the cereal box must come off to do this.

One way to get around this is to set the camera to record video rather than having it in 'still' mode. This is more memory-intensive, but it does mean the camera won't shut off as long as there is still free memory; many phones will have more than enough even for a long playing session.

You can easily delete the video afterwards – or keep it to relive your robotic experiences.

It isn't only walking that's difficult. Picking up objects and placing them accurately is also very tricky while wearing the RCBVS. Exploit this robot weakness and include some manual work in your obstacle course, with cereal-boxed players having to grab hold of something and bring it back to the starting point.

Robot relay race

For a relay race, you will need two RCBVS-equipped cereal boxes. Each team splits into two, with half of the players at each end of the course. When the first player completes one leg of the course he or she hands over the RCBVS and the 'baton' (use a raw egg for maximum trickiness) to their team mate, who must put on the cereal box and race back through the course in reverse, handing over to the next player, and so on.

From the archives...

Charades
The most efficaceous family game ever devised.

In Charades, a player is given the title of a book, film, song, play or other entertainment. They must enact this without using any words.

To begin, the player indicates the number of words in the title by holding up the same number of fingers. They also 'tell' their audience what form of entertainment the title represents, as follows:

1. **For a book**, hold both hands as if reading a weighty tome.
2. **For a film**, mime turning the handle on an old-fashioned crank film camera.
3. **For a song**, mime an opera singer.
4. **For a play**, mime curtains parting.

A play　　　　*A film*

The player can then either perform a mime that represents the whole title, or break it down into individual words and syllables.

Fingers are held up to indicate which word is being enacted, and fingers placed on the arm to show how many syllables there are in the word, and which syllable is about to be mimed.

If a player is unable to mime a word, he can hold a hand to his ear to perform a mime that 'sounds like' the word.

Two words　　　　*Three syllables*

Small words such as 'a', 'the' or 'of' may be indicated by holding two fingers close together, while a name is indicated by tapping one's head with the open hand (gentlemen may wish to remove their headgear in advance of this).

Small word　　　　*A name*

Whoever guesses the title correctly is the next player to perform a mime. The title is given to them by the previous player, either whispered or written on paper.

A variation

Some people prefer to play Charades in two teams, with each player performing the mime to their own team only. The drawback with this version is that at any time half the players are not playing the game, but simply watching.

The hat game

A name-guessing for adults and children.

To play The Hat Game, begin by tearing or cutting a sheet of paper into small strips.

Each player has three to five strips, on which they write the name of a person, living, dead, or fictional. All the strips are folded in half and placed into a hat. The players are divided into two teams.

Round one

In the first round, one player takes a name at random from the hat and must get the rest of his team to guess who it is. They can speak, but must not say the name of the person on the paper.

A player may reject a name and draw out another at any stage should they find themselves thwarted by their team's ineptitude. Once a name is guessed, the player puts the paper to one side and retrieves another name from the hat.

Play continues for one minute, as timed by the other team, after which the hat is passed to a member of the opposing team, who must themselves then act out as many names as possible in one minute.

Round two

Once all the names have been correctly guessed, the strips of paper are counted for each team's score, and then are all returned to the hat.

Players again pluck names at random and have to get their teammates to guess who they are. This time, though, they are only allowed to speak *a single word*. They are, however, permitted to use actions to help their team members arrive at the answer.

Round three

After round two is complete, the strips are counted and added to each team's score once again.

The third round proceeds exactly as before, except that this time *players are not allowed to speak at all*. All the clues must be given through mime alone.

Do not lose heart: although words are forbidden, the players' task is greatly facilitated through having already seen all the names twice, in the previous rounds.

At the end of the round, the slips are counted and the final scores totted up.

Game tactics

As seasoned players will be aware, the way to win this game is to give visual clues from the outset, while speech is still permitted. So, if one of the names is, say, 'Admiral Nelson', the player should mime a one-eyed man with a telescope.

2+
Players

Indoor/Outdoor

Construction

Active

Mobile phone

Eye, Robot 2

Yet more diminished vision fun using our invented Robot Cereal Box Vision System™.

SET UP 10 mins | **PLAY TIME 20+ mins** | **YOU NEED** an empty cereal box • a camera phone

These games use a camera phone taped to the bottom of an empty cereal box – see page 222 for how this is done. Remember to use the larger size cereal boxes. The smaller ones are too tight and, particularly when adults are using them, are likely to give some peripheral vision and thus ruin the fun.

Robot exterminator

For this game you will need a fairly large playing area with clearly defined boundaries: a garden is the obvious place, unless you happen to have a huge living room with no breakable objects. One player is the robot, and wears the Robot Cereal Box Vision System (RCBVS) on his head. Out of sight of the robot, the other players put on different coloured hats or scarves.

The non-robot players position themselves around the playing area, then the RCBVS robot enters. The robot's aim is to correctly identify all the other players. They do this by stating not only the player's name but also the item they are wearing, as in: 'I see you, Steve, with the yellow woolly hat'. The aim of the players, of course, is to avoid being identified, by leaping out of the robot's field of vision.

For maximum dramatic effect, the robot should use a suitably scary voice. A fun variation is to force correctly identified players to freeze so the robot can creepily advance and 'exterminate' them by touching them with his finger. You'd be surprised how sinister somebody can seem with a cereal box on their head!

The last player left standing is the winner, and swaps place with the robot for the next round.

Zoom challenge

Even with the camera set at normal zoom, performing tasks while wearing our robot eyes can be tricky. If you zoom to maximum, however, things that are usually simple can become seriously difficult.

Here are a few things you can order a robot with zoomed-in vision to do. (Spectators should keep a safe distance while they laugh hysterically at the robot's clumsy fumblings – just in case it still has its Dalek-like extermination powers left over from the last game.)

- Pick up a glass of water and pour it into another glass

- Grasp grains of rice with chopsticks or tweezers

- Shake hands with the other people in the room

- Throw a ball up with one hand and catch it

- Juggle. (We think this might be not only difficult, but impossible – especially since one hand is needed to hold the box.)

Robot jousting

If you have two camera phones, then make up two RCBVS devices, one for each player.

The players are armed with a sword each, and have to try to stab each other while wearing the cereal box – it's harder than it sounds.

We find that this game becomes considerably less fun if you use real swords or daggers: instead try thick sheets of cardboard or, better, some pipe lagging bought from a hardware store.

THREE LAWS

The title **I, Robot** comes from a book by Isaac Asimov, written in 1950. This was the first book to outline the Three Laws of Robotics:

1. A robot may not injure a human being or, through inaction, allow a human being to come to harm.

2. A robot must obey any orders given to it by human beings, except where such orders would conflict with the First Law.

3. A robot must protect its own existence as long as such protection does not conflict with the First or Second Law.

Invented your own great new game using Robot Vision? Let everyone know.

fg-21.com/forum

25

Food Facts Top Trumps

Defeat your opponents, not with cards, but with the contents of your kitchen cupboard.

| SET UP 10 mins | PLAY TIME 20+ mins | YOU NEED packs or tins of food |

The card game *Top Trumps* has been around since 1977, each pack based around a topic like racing cars, footballers, or the latest movie blockbuster.

Our version dispenses with the cards altogether, instead using the nutritional information found on most food packaging. We've amended the original *Top Trumps* rules to cater (ha ha) for the fact that most families won't want to ransack the entire contents of their kitchen to play the game.

Nutrition information

As part of its efforts to get the nation to eat more healthily, the government encourages manufacturers to label food products with nutritional information, listed as a value per 100g. From this you can find out how much energy, protein, carbohydrate, fat, fibre, sodium and salt is present, with the carbohydrate category usually specifying how much is sugar and the fat category divided into saturated and unsaturated.

All very handy, no doubt, in helping people choose what food to buy. But far more useful, in our opinion, for playing Food Facts Top Trumps.

Setting up

Each player collects four items of food. They can be packets, tins or jars, as long as they have a standard Nutritional Information label on the back. They are placed in the middle of the table with the information panels facing down. All the players sit around the table.

How to play

1. Each player starts by taking a single item of food from the pile. The first player – perhaps the youngest – picks the food element that they think will have a value higher than on anyone else's packs. They read out its value per 100 gms, as in: 'sodium, 676 mg'.

2. Going clockwise, each player in turn then announces the value for the same ingredient on their own pack.

3. Whoever has the pack with the highest value wins the round. Whoever has the lowest value hands their pack to the winner, and chooses something else from the pile in the middle of the table.

4. If a food element isn't listed on a player's pack, or if it's listed as 'trace', they pass on that round, and neither gain nor lose a pack.

5. The player to the left of the previous starter begins the next round, choosing the food element which they think will score highest.

6. If a player has two or more food items (because they've won items from other players), they may choose which item to use – without, however, checking in advance.

7. When there are no more packs left in the middle of the table, play continues for one further round. The player who then has the most food items wins the game.

Geocaching: getting started

Revive your love of the great outdoors by taking part in the new global GPS-based treasure hunt phenomenon.

1+

Players

Outdoor

Active

GPS device

| SET UP 30 mins | PLAY TIME 1+ hrs | YOU NEED a SatNav device or GPS phone |

This worldwide treasure-hunting activity can be engaged in anywhere, in towns and cities as well as in the country. Over a million caches have been hidden all around the world, including in Antarctica, ready to be found by people guided by satellite-controlled location devices. There's even one on the International Space Station.

Although there are plenty of solitary geocachers, it is such a great group activity that even lethargic family members can be coaxed into walks and trips into the unknown. Geocaching is very much a 21st-century hobby, only beginning in 2000 after the American military stopped jamming civilian GPS devices.

What you need

Dedicated GPS devices cost from £70 upwards, but many modern mobile phones, such as the iPhone, are also GPS-equipped. You should also register as a member on *www.geocaching.com*. Basic membership is free and provides all you need to get started. But even if you get hooked by the geocaching bug, full membership only costs $30 a year. You'll also need a pen and transport. Many caches are in out-of-the-way places, often favoured haunts of those who hide them.

Finding your first cache

On the geocaching.com website, find the 'Hide & Seek a Cache' section. Enter your own postcode or a location you plan travelling to. You'll find a variety of caches hidden in the area, together with the distance and direction from your starting point. The D/T column tells you how *Difficult* it might be to find each cache, and how *Tough* the

A typical cache, with an assortment of items left by previous visitors.

NO SATNAV?

If you don't yet have a GPS device and are not sure whether you will enjoy geocaching, try using a map instead to begin with. To get your bearings, adapt the GPS coordinates and enter them into an online map system like Google Maps or streetmap.co.uk.

It won't be as accurate as GPS, of course, but if the difficulty rating is low, you should be able to find the treasure anyway.

terrain will be (the space station is 5/5). Obviously, for a first cache, you should try something relatively easy.

Each entry has information about the location and, depending on how difficult the cacher wants to make it, a hint or two as to what you will be looking for. The most important information is the coordinates, which should be entered into the GPS device (you can do this automatically. The geocaching.com website also explains what you'll need for 'paperless geocaching'.

What to expect

The GPS coordinates will get you to within 10-20 feet of the cache, which will be hidden in a weatherproof plastic or metal container. Inside you'll find a guest log, a 'visitors book', which you should sign and date to show when you found it. There'll probably also be some sort of trinket which you are welcome to take, etiquette dictating that you should replace the 'swag' with something of the same or greater value. Sometimes there's a disposable camera – take a picture of yourselves and put it back in. Leave everything just as you found it, and when you get home, record your visit on the geocaching.com website.

Age 8+

Geocaching: going further

1+

Players

You've found your first cache – now take the GPS treasure hunt to the next level.

Outdoor

| SET UP 30 mins | PLAY TIME 1+ hrs | YOU NEED a SatNav device or GPS phone |

As you'll soon discover, geocachers tend to have fertile imaginations and like to make life interesting for hunters. For instance, there are 'multi-caches' with several stages, with the first cache giving information about the next and so on.

Active

Or a set of coordinates may not mark a cache at all, but the location of a puzzle that must be solved in order to complete the quest and find the treasure. These range from simple to brain-teasingly cryptic. You may, for instance, be required to use your ingenuity to decode the text on a tombstone or a monument.

We came across one called 'Poor Tiddles'. After hunting in vain for a clue or a cache, the hunter finally twigged that two telephone numbers on a poster of a missing cat weren't real phone numbers, but GPS coordinates.

GPS device

Hiding your first cache

Once you've found a few caches, you will no longer be a newbie and may well feel the urge to place one of your own.

Bear in mind that you will be responsible for maintaining it, and that you may need the permission of a landowner. The Geocaching Association of Great Britain (*www.gagb.org.uk*), which is free to join, maintains a database of landowners and organisations that have given blanket approval for caches to be hidden on their property, along with those who haven't. So while you're fine in Brecon Beacons National Park, you should steer clear of London's Royal Parks.

Obviously, nothing dangerous should ever be hidden in a cache, and food should also be avoided. Not only might it attract wildlife, but if the cache remains undiscovered for some time, there will be a nasty surprise for whoever does eventually find it. It is also wise to steer clear of government buildings or anywhere where people might misconstrue geocaching as suspicious activity.

There are tens of thousands of UK geocachers, who refer to the uninitiated as 'muggles' – a term borrowed from the Harry Potter books. If a civilian steals or spoils a cache, you've been 'muggled'.

If you don't want to maintain a cache any longer, rather than simply retrieving it and deleting it from the geocaching.com database, you can put it up for 'adoption' and see if anyone else would like to take it on.

Travelling caches

Not all caches are stationary. They may contain a 'travel bug' or 'geocoin'. These are known as 'trackables' – treasure that the owners hope cachers will remove and place in another cache. Some travel bugs are aimless wanderers, but sometimes the owners specify where they would like them to end up – it's amazing how far some have voyaged.

Trackables have a unique ID and their movements are recorded online, so you can follow the journey of any that you have been involved with. And of course, you can always launch a travel bug of your very own.

Some geocaches are very small, and can be well hidden.

LANGUAGE

The international geocaching logo is shown above.

Here are some useful geocaching acronyms:

TFTC Thanks for the cache.

TNLN Took nothing, left nothing.

SL Signed log

BYOP Bring your own pen.

CITO Cache in, trash out. Geocaching etiquette says you should tidy up rubbish after finding a cache.

FTF First to find

DNF Did not find.

TB Travel bug.

URP Unnatural rock pile. A common method of disguising caches.

Age 11+

2+

Players

Indoor

Brain power

Computer

Google Earth challenge

Do you know your Taj Mahal from your Machu Picchu? Find out by taking our Google Earth Challenge.

| SET UP 2+ mins | PLAY TIME 15+ mins | YOU NEED a computer with internet access |

The application Google Earth is a fascinating way to explore the planet from the air. We've come up with a challenge where players have to try to identify landmarks from around the world.

Setting up

You'll need to download a copy of Google Earth. It's available for Macs and PCs, it's free, and you can get it here:

http://earth.google.co.uk/

We've set up a tour that features ten landmarks, and will pause at each one for long enough for you to have a crack at identifying it. The tour is a plug-in file for Google Earth, and you can download it here:

fg-21.com/tour.kmz

Open Google Earth and make sure all the various overlays in the left sidebar are unchecked. If you don't do this, you'll see markers showing the name of each place, which will spoil the game. Then double-click the file you've downloaded, and the tour will start to run.

Playing the game

The tour zooms around the world, visiting each of the landmarks in turn. If you need longer to study each one, you can pause the tour using the on-screen controller:

Google Earth images © Google, Bluesky, Sanborn, DigitalGlobe, GeoEye, Aerodata International Surveys, Infoterra, TerraMetrics

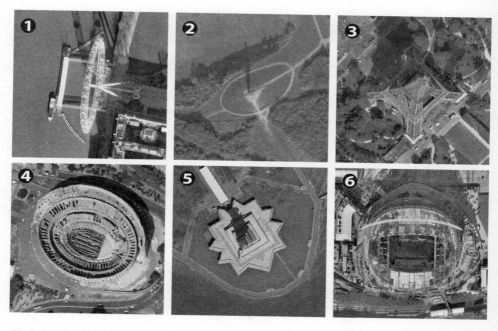

Click the Play/Pause button, second from the left, to stop and restart the tour. If the controller isn't visible, move your cursor to the bottom left portion of the Google Earth window and it should pop into view. There is also the option of zooming in further, before continuing the tour when you're done.

Printed above are six of the landmarks from the tour. Can you identify them all? Some are harder to work out when photographed from directly above, but their shadows should give you a clue. Answers are printed below.

GOING FURTHER

We've provided a tour for you to download, but you can easily make your own using Google Earth — see page 216.

Created your own Google Earth challenge? Try it out on others.

1. The London Eye; 2. The Angel of the North; 3. The Eiffel Tower; 4. The Coliseum; 5. The Statue of Liberty; 6. Wembley Stadium.

fg-21.com/forum

All ages

2+

Players

Outdoor

Active

Guided missile golf

Play golf anywhere without balls or clubs – and you don't have to wear silly trousers either.

SET UP 10 mins | **PLAY TIME** 15+ mins | **YOU NEED** a blindfold for each 'ball' player

This golf game needs no clubs or balls, only an even number of participants and some blindfolds. Unlike the real thing, it's almost as much fun for the spectators as it is for the players.

Setting up

Whether in your garden, in a park or at the beach, mark out a course consisting of a series of 'holes', each of which has a start point (the tee) and a finishing point (the flag). There can be as many or as few holes as you like. The starting tee can be marked with anything – a twig or a stick will do fine. The finishing flag should be a circle a few inches across. One easy way to make this is to poke a stick or pencil through a paper plate to fix it into the ground – or just use a hula hoop.

The distance from tee to flag can be anywhere from 5 to 50 metres or even longer, depending how much space you have. We recommend varying the length of your holes for a more interesting course.

Divide the players into pairs. One is the golfer, and the other is the golfball. The golfball needs to be blindfolded so they can't see where they're going (see page 223).

Teeing off

The golfer starts by leading the golfball to the teeing-off position. He or she then aims the golfball towards the hole and tells them how many steps they should take. This counts as one 'shot'.

The golfball takes the stated number of steps in the direction in which they're facing, and stops. If they're in the hole at the first attempt, that's a hole in one. If, as is more likely, they are not, the golfer must re-aim them and give them a new number of paces to take. If there is more than one golfball-golfer pair, they take it in turn to take 'shots'.

Once the ball is within 'putting' distance, the golfer may specify that they take shorter, heel-to-toe steps. The score for the hole is the number of times the ball is given instructions by the golfer before reaching the hole.

When the course is completed, the scores for all the individual holes are totalled, the winner, as in golf, being the pair with the lowest score.

Adding obstacles

The game can be refined further by adding bunkers. If you don't fancy digging a big hole in your lawn, just sprinkle some sand from your sandpit on the grass, or lay an old sheet or rug down to represent the sand instead.

If a golfball ends up in a bunker, they must jump clear with the next shot. In this case, the golfer should turn the ball in the right direction, as with a normal shot, then instruct them to 'Jump!'

GOING FURTHER

Add even more variety to your course by introducing 'dog-leg' holes with a bend in them — ensuring the 'ball' avoids injury by walking slowly with arms outstretched in front of them.

The really dedicated 'guided missile golfer' can create a score card for their course, showing distances and 'par' scores for each hole. You'll find plenty of examples of real golf scorecards online.

1+

Players

Indoor

Active

Hairdryer ping pong

Fly a ping pong ball by remote control, and guide it through the obstacles.

SET UP 10 mins | PLAY TIME 15+ mins | YOU NEED ping pong ball, hairdryer, coat hangers

If you hold a hairdryer so that it's blowing upwards and let go of a ping pong ball just a few inches above the nozzle, it will stay in the airstream, bobbling gently. You can tilt the hairdryer some way away from the vertical and the ping pong ball still won't drop out of the flowing air.

The reason, should anyone be curious enough to ask, is the Bernoulli Effect. There are some excellent demonstrations on YouTube.

What it means in practice is that you can press the hairdryer into service for some interesting games.

Stay cool

Given the heat that a hairdryer puts out, you might want to operate it on the cool setting. It's better for the environment and little kids' fingers. There's also less chance of the ping pong ball melting.

Buckets of balls

Give a player a dozen ping pong balls and a starting point. See how many balls they can get to drop into a target bowl or bucket. It is surprisingly hard to predict at what point gravity will reassert its authority and cause a ball to fall. To vary the difficulty of the challenge, change the size of the target receptacle.

Obstacle course

This takes a little more preparation, but is worth the effort. The simplest obstacles to set up are coat hangers. These can easily be wedged between books, leaving a vertical 'hoop' for the ball to pass through. Time how long it takes people to navigate the ball around the course.

If you want to do more Bernoulli Effect experiments, try this.

Use tape to attach a couple of ping pong balls to lengths of string or thread, and dangle them level but a few inches apart.

Point the hairdryer at them and, instead of moving further apart as you might expect, they draw together.

As another experiment, place a ping pong ball in your hand, and blow hard onto it through a funnel, with the wide end down. Surprisingly, the ball will be sucked upwards.

It is also fun to arrange the hangers horizontally (put the hook under the books rather than between them). See how many times you can get the ball to go up through the hanger and back down outside it. We find that both this and the vertical hoop version are easier with wire hangers than the thick plastic sort, which disrupt the airflow and should only be attempted by advanced players.

When you plan your obstacle course, remember that you're limited by the length of the flex on the hairdryer, unless you're prepared to use an extension cord (in which case you're still limited by that, of course).

Variation

Balloons work as well as ping pong balls, so have a go at these games with them too. You may find the coat hangers are too small to serve as hoops, though.

Age 8+

2+

Players

Indoor/Outdoor

Digital camera

Happy snappy

Use camera phones and a little imagination to set up treasure hunts in a trice wherever you are.

SET UP 10 mins | PLAY TIME 15+ mins | YOU NEED digital cameras

Every modern mobile now includes a camera, which means a phone is all you need for a modern scavenger hunt. Instead of collecting the objects themselves, the scavengers simply photograph them.

This game is infinitely adaptable: you can play it indoors or out, with just one child or with a whole party-full of them. If there aren't enough phones to go around, group players into teams.

Preparing a camera scavenger hunt

Come up with suitable lists of 'treasure' to be found and photographed. For a party group, print them out in advance.

In the home, this might include:

- A teaspoon
- A particular DVD
- A pair of white shoes
- A cereal box
- A pillow
- A newspaper
- Somebody using a camera
- A calendar

Outside, you might suggest things like these:

- A pigeon
- A litter bin
- A red car
- A street sign
- A bicycle
- A post box
- A warning sign
- A drain

The first back with every item photographed is the winner. These camera treasure hunt games are particularly good for that deadeningly dull time spent hanging about in airports after you've checked in. It's easy to come up with an appropriate list.

Lateral photography

If you want players to use their imaginations a little more, come up with topics instead of specific lists, asking them, for instance, to photograph things that are 'round' or 'heavy' or 'old'.

For 'round', the sort of things they might capture are:

- A biscuit
- A tin lid
- A tyre
- A ring
- A flower
- A clock
- An eyeball
- A roll of Sellotape

Or you could just ask for items beginning with 'A', or for things that are white, or things that are in the wrong place, and so on.

Who's the winner?

It can be tiresome having to go through all the photos, ticking them off, particularly if a large group is playing. Instead, group the players together and ask them, one by one, to name an object they've photographed. If anybody else has shot a picture of the same thing, all those photos should be deleted.

At the end each player counts up their unique photographs, with the winner being the one who took the greatest number.

Camera spelling bee

Another variation, ideally suited to the airport, is to get players to take photos of objects whose first letters spell out words. So pictures of a camera, an advert and a trolley would make the word 'cat'. Who can come up with the longest word? If you have a *really* long wait, set them the 'antidisestablishmentarianism' camera spelling bee challenge.

Part of the fun here is listening to the children's justifications. Can that person in uniform really be called an 'airport cleaner', for instance?

GOING FURTHER

Photograph three objects. Show them to the children but in a zoomed-in form. If they can find and photograph the item they get 3 points. If not, they can return to see it zoomed out a little more but will only get 2 points.

Return a second time and they can see it zoomed out completely but they will only get 1 point if they find and photograph it.

10+

Players

Indoor

Party game

Active

HipSync

Synchronise your dancing with others – while wearing plastic lips.

SET UP 45 mins | **PLAY TIME 20+ mins** | **YOU NEED** mp3 players • plastic lips

This party game, devised by Duncan Speakman and Simon Johnson, is often played at social occasions for adults, but works equally well for children's parties and family gatherings.

Since the players wear headphones, it can be played even in a noisy environment. And the opposite is also true: it's one of those rare children's party games that is silent for those not playing, which gives the adults a welcome break from the noise of kids having fun.

Setting up

Ask your guests to bring mp3 players and headphones (making sure they will be able identify them afterwards). In advance of the party, the party boy or girl must come up with a list of five songs that everybody already has, or can easily get hold of. Players will need to put these into a separate party playlist on their mp3 players. The songs chosen must all be of different durations, ideally by at least 10 seconds.

You must also provide as many sets of false plastic lips as there are players.

How to play

A controller, in charge of the game, assigns each player one of the songs, together with a set of false lips so that they can't talk.

Ensuring that everyone is watching, the controller counts down from five seconds. On the count of zero, everyone presses 'play' on their mp3 player, and starts to dance to their song. The aim is to find other players who are listening to the same song and partner up with them. As soon as their song ends, players must stop dancing and put

This game was first published on the website ludocity.com.

up their hands. Anyone dancing on their own, or in a group without any other players with their hand up, is knocked out. (Remember: those listening to other songs won't yet have their hands raised, since all the songs are of different durations.)

New songs are assigned for the next round and off they go again. This is a great spectator game, which softens the blow for those knocked out early on.

Duelling dancers

The game can also be played as a succession of duels between pairs of dancers. Each sports a pair of plastic lips, as well as an mp3 player, with the playlist of five songs set to shuffle mode.

The controller starts the dancers as before, but this time uses a stopwatch to time their efforts to get in sync.

The players must skip through the five tracks until they both believe they are dancing to the same song. They then raise their hands and stop their mp3 players.

If they are indeed both on the same track, their time is logged. The pair who 'HipSync' quickest are the winners.

SING A SONG

A singing teacher friend told us that when you sing along to music with headphones on, you really can't tell how you sound. Even decent singers stray comically from the musical straight and narrow. Note this only works with old-style headphones that totally envelope the ear, not the in-ear bud variety.

In this game, each person chooses a song. They are recorded as they sing along, trying to ignore the laughter of the audience. They must then listen back to a minimum of 30 seconds of their crooning.

Share your best HipSync playlists on our forum.

fg-21.com/forum

41

Age 11+

How to Googlewhack

The classic Google game that gets ever more fiendish.

SET UP 2 mins | PLAY TIME 15+ mins | YOU NEED computer with internet

1+
Players

Indoor

Brain power

Computer

Stick two words into Google and set it searching. How many results do you get? Hundreds? Thousands? Millions? How low can you get this figure? That's the idea behind a Googlewhack. It's a search query in which two words give only one result. In other words, those two words appear on only one website anywhere in the world.

It was invented by Gary Stock in 2001, who set up the website googlewhack.com to register people's Googlewhacks. Sadly, by declaring a Googlewhack online, you automatically double the number of websites it appears on, and so your Googlewhack is no more. The Googlewhack is the mayfly of the cybersphere.

Rules for Googlewhacking

The two words must appear exactly as written, must not appear in 'word lists' (such as online dictionary summaries) and must not be entered within quotation marks.

Advice for Googlewhackers

Start with an unusual word. We chose *axolotl*, a kind of salamander. To this, we tried pairing *hydrochloric*, only to discover that axolotls are routinely treated with dilute hydrochloric acid in the dissection process. The upshot? 2,230 results.

We tried unlikely compound words. *Axolotl* and *dishbanana* got a single result, but Google suggested dishbanana should be two words and, in the only entry it found, dish and banana were separated by a full stop, so it didn't count.

We tried that old favourite, *antidisestablishmentarianism* (the political ideology that holds that church and state should not be separated).

42

Pausing for breath after typing it, we combined it with *axolotl*. 3,280 results, including, bizarrely, someone who had named their pet axolotl Antidisestablishmentarianism. A frustrated Googlewhacker perhaps.

How about upping the 'anti' and trying just *disestablishmentarianism*, combined with *axolotl*? Only 350 results. Getting better.

Disestablishmentarianist looked even more promising but Google's search initially showed us *disestablishmentarianism* too, so we had to specify we didn't want variations of the word (see 'Going Further' in the sidebar to find out how do this).

Finally, a Googlewhack!

With heavy hearts, we decided to ditch the axolotl and focus on *disestablishmentarianist*. We examined the sites Google proffered to see if any contained unusual words. In *Wired* magazine was an obituary of the world's oldest punk rocker – 80-year-old Joseph Zak. Not only was he a notable disestablishmentarianist but also, 'The world's first punk rock graphomaniac'.

With growing excitement, we entered *disestablishmentarianist* and *graphomaniac* together. Just a single result – our first Googlewhack!

---

disestablismentarianist graphomaniac   Search

1 result (0.20 seconds)   Advanced search

The Death of the World's Oldest Punk Rocker | Table Of Malcontents
29 Dec 2006 ... than screaming out your guttural **disestablishmentarianist** screams, ... The world's first punk rock **graphomaniac**! Mr. Zak has no family, ...
www.wired.com/table_of_malcontents/2006/12/the_death_of_th/ - Cached

---

GOING FURTHER

When searching in Google, use a minus sign immediately before a word to specify that you want that word to be excluded.

Putting a + sign immediately before a word means you do not want any variations of it. Enclose a phrase in inverted commas if you only want examples of that complete phrase as you typed it.

Found a new Googlewhack? Don't keep it to yourself — share it!

fg-21.com/forum

43

From the archives...

Flipping kipper

*Be the first to flip your
kipper off the table.*

Cut out fish shapes from pieces of thin paper, one for each player. They should be about 20cm long.

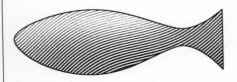

Line up all the kippers at one end of a table. Players must race their kipper to the other edge of the table, creating a draught by flapping a piece of card or a magazine.

Wink murder

*Can you unmask the secret
killer in your family?*

Prepare as many small pieces of paper as there are players, and write an X on one of them. Fold them in half, and place into a hat.

Each player takes one paper from the hat, and opens it in secret. The one with the X is the murderer.

When the murderer thinks no one is looking, they have to 'kill' the other players by winking at them. If a player sees the murderer winking at someone else, he has been found out and loses the game.

Cheat

*A card game involving
bluff and deception.*

Deal out two packs of cards so each player has a roughly equal number. The players should then sort their own cards by number – the suits don't matter.

The first player places a number of cards, supposedly of the same value, face down on the table, declaring what they are – 'three eights', for example. They are, however, permitted to lie.

The next player must put down any number of cards, either of the same value, or one rank higher or lower. So as well as eights, they may choose sevens or nines.

The aim of the game is for a player to get rid of all their cards.

If one player suspects another of cheating, they call 'Cheat!'. The player who put down the last set of cards must turn them over.

If they did cheat, they take all the cards on the table and add them to their hand; if they, on the other hand, did place the cards claimed, the player who called 'Cheat!' must pick up all the cards.

Eat the jelly

*A party game for
younger players.*

Each player takes it in turn to throw a die (or make your own talking computer dice – see page 208).

As soon as one player throws a 6, they must put on mittens, a scarf and a hat, and each as much jelly from a plate as they can, but they're only permitted to use a knife and fork.

When the next player throws a 6, the hat, scarf and mittens pass to them.

Balloonatics

*Pass the balloon from player
to player, using only knees.*

For this children's party game you require thin, elongated balloons rather than the more bulbous sort generally in use.

Divide players into two equal teams, who stand in line next to each other. Give the players at the head of the lines a balloon, which they grip between their knees.

Using only their knees, they pass the balloon to the next player, and they to the next, all the way down the line to the end.

French cricket

The perfect outdoor game.

One player is 'in', and holds a cricket bat in front of their legs. The other players stand in a ring around them and take turns to bowl a tennis ball, underarm, trying to hit the batsman's legs.

Should the batsman miss the ball, they're not allowed to turn around to face the next throw.

A player is 'out' when the ball hits their legs beneath the knee (in which case the bowler is 'in') or when a player catches the ball after the batsman has hit it (in which case the catcher is 'in').

Tin can phone

*A telephone made from
two empty cans.*

Take two empty tins and wash them to remove all traces of baked beans, cat food, mulligatawny soup or whatever.

Make a small hole in the end of each, and thread a string between them. When pulled taut, if someone speaks into one can they can be heard clearly in the other. This works even with long strings, up to about 50 yards – almost a quarter of a furlong.

Car game

Human SatNav

Kids provide the navigation as they guide the driver in the manner of a SatNav.

| SET UP 1 min | PLAY TIME 30+ mins | YOU NEED a driver with a lot of patience |

You've gone out for the day but, on reaching your destination, it's raining so hard you can't face getting out of the car. Turn the engine back on and let the kids play the part of a SatNav device, taking you on a mystery tour.

It's a modern version of the steering wheel with a suction cup we had as kids, pretending to drive from the back seat.

How to play

If you already have a SatNav, the family should be only too familiar with the sort of instructions it gives: 'At the end of the road, turn right'; 'After 100 yards, turn left'; 'At the roundabout, take the third exit', and so on.

One child should start giving instructions using the language of a SatNav, and whoever is driving the car must follow them, unless they are being ordered the wrong way down a one-way street or to do anything else illegal. Even if the driver knows they are being routed into a dead end, they should still do what they are told. The next instruction should then be: 'Turn around when possible.'

Changing the SatNav

If there is more than one player, the person playing the SatNav should switch if they utter any language or behaviour inappropriate to a calm and well-mannered, not to say robotic SatNav system – such as laughing, hesitating, saying 'Um', 'Er', 'Yes', 'No', 'Mum', 'Dad', or yelling out 'I didn't mean here, I meant there!' A judge should be appointed at the outset whose decision is final. Should a player be doing so well that the

At the end of the road... er...

GOING FURTHER

You don't have to wait for rain to stop play. Try it on the last leg of any journey back home. How well do the kids know the route? The winner is the person playing the SatNav when you reach home.

non-players are getting restless, make it more difficult by having them do it in a Scottish or Russian accent, or add the word 'pig' to every instruction without laughing.

If you arrive somewhere lovely and the rain stops, call an end to the game, the winner being the last person to be the SatNav.

The twist in the tail

If you feel you've been driving long enough, have the SatNav impersonators attempt to guide you back to your starting point. How well will the children remember the route taken, and can they get you back again? It is quite possible that you will get horribly lost playing this game, in which case you'll be glad if you have a real SatNav.

IM a teapot

Play word games with friends or family anywhere in the world – for free.

| SET UP 2 mins | PLAY TIME 10+ mins | YOU NEED computers with IM programs |

Instant messaging lets you have real-time text 'conversations' with your friends, however many miles separate you.

These games can be played with friends, of course, but are also a great way for parents who are away to spend some fun time with their children before bedtime.

Some IM services, like Apple's **iChat** and **Skype**, restrict text chats to two people a time, as does **Facebook**. A few, like **Windows Live Messenger** (formerly called **MSN Messenger**) let you chat with larger groups, in this case a maximum of 20. Players don't have to be on opposite sides of the planet. With two computers, there's no reason why they can't be in the same house.

Cheddar Gorge

In this game, popularised on Radio 4's comedy panel game *I'm Sorry I Haven't A Clue*, two players string a sentence out for as long as possible by producing alternate words. The first player forced to finish the sentence loses that round.

One player sets the topic, such as 'What I did last Thursday' or 'How to tie a shoelace'. The next player begins by typing the first word.

The sentence will become unwieldy and possibly nonsensical, but that's part of the fun, as each player tries to trap the other into typing a concluding word.

Psychiatrist

Movie and TV psychiatrists often say a word and ask their patients what immediately comes to mind. It's something pioneering psychi-

GOING FURTHER

These games can be also be played out loud as face-to-face games.

Conversely, several of the other games in this book, most notably car games (pages 64-67) can be played as IM games.

Most social networking sites have a range of readymade online games, our favourites being **Scrabble** and **Lexulous** on Facebook.

atrist Karl Jung thought up, claiming that it would reveal something deeply interesting about people's subconscious.

Whether that's true or not, rapid word association makes a great game for two or more. Players type out words in turn. The sequence might go: 'monkey', 'nut', 'shell', 'missile' and so on. If somebody produces a word that seems to have no connection with the previous one, any player can challenge them. However, a challenge carries risks. If the other players consider the association perfectly valid, the challenger is out of that round.

With only two players, one can ask the other to explain an association but there's no way of policing who is right – unless you call in a psychiatrist, of course.

Morph

The first player begins with any four-letter word. The other players must produce further four-letter words in turn, by changing just one letter at a time. So 'boot' might become 'book' and then 'cook', which could then become 'cool', and so on.

When a player can't come up with a word that has not yet been used, they are out of that round.

Age 11+

2+
Players

Indoor

Remote friends

IM still a teapot

Games for older players using Instant Messaging online chat systems.

SET UP 2 mins | PLAY TIME 15+ mins | YOU NEED computers with IM programs

Instant Messaging games can also be fun for older players. These require a little more thought than those on the preceding pages.

As with the earlier games, these can also be played face to face.

Carnelli

This association game was invented by American Mensa member Jan Carnell and uses connections in the titles of books, movies, plays or songs. They might be plays by the same dramatist, books with words in common, or films starring the same actor or with the same director.

So *The Empire Strikes Back* could be followed by *Star Wars* (both directed by George Lucas) or *Raiders of the Lost Ark* (both starring Harrison Ford), or *The Last Emperor* or even *Back to the Future* (they have words in common). If *Star Wars* was chosen, the next association might be *A Star Is Born*, and so on.

Puns and wordplay are encouraged. *Camelot*, for example, could be followed by *Lawrence of Arabia*, because it's a film with 'a lot of camels'. Players can be challenged to explain their reasoning. When

played in a group in the same room, it is usual to have one person adjudicating. Online, the group as a whole should decide if they think a challenged association is fair.

Endless Words

Players type a letter at a time, always having a word in mind. The aim is to avoid ever completing a word. So if a player is faced with 'creat', rather than ending the word with an 'e' to make 'create', they might add an 'i' to give 'creati', thinking of 'creation'. But the next letter could be 'v', making 'creativ', with the player hoping the next person will have to put down 'creative'.

However, instead, they could add an 'i' so that it now reads 'creativi'. The next player will put 't' to make 'creativit', hoping trap their opponent into putting 'creativity'; but a really crafty player will escape by adding not a game-ending 'y', but an 'i' as part of 'creativities'.

If a player does not believe that the last person to go has a valid word in mind, or they feel that their last move completed a *bona fide* word, they may issue a challenge. If a challenge is successful, the person challenged loses a life. If it's wrong, the challenger loses one. The game ends when all but one player has lost three lives.

Tail to Head

Pick a topic, which may be something general like 'animals' or more specialised, like 'TV shows'. One player starts it off by typing a word in that category. Other players follow, but each word must start with the last letter of the previous word. So *The Simpsons* might be followed by *Scrapheap Challenge*, and so on.

A time limit of 10 seconds should be imposed; anyone not producing a word in time is out. With the clock ticking, it's amazing how empty your brain can get.

GOING FURTHER

A neat variation of the Endless Words game is to allow players to add letters at the beginning of the word, as well as at the end.

This makes it a much trickier business altogether. See how your opponents fare if you open with the letter combination 'ghsh' – will they realise it's the middle section of 'roughshod'?

Have you come up with your own Instant Messaging games? Spread the word.

fg-21.com/forum

Age 8+

2+
Players

Car game

Digital camera

iSpied

A jazzed-up 21st-century version of the game played by our Stone Age ancestors.

SET UP 2 mins | **PLAY TIME 1+ hr** | **YOU NEED** a digital camera or camera phone

While some adults may like spending rainy afternoons wandering around stately homes and museums, most kids crash through their boredom threshold the same instant they crash through the turnstile.

This game will keep them interested, so that they will actually enjoy looking around, and trying to remember everything they see.

On the outing

Each player has a digital camera, or a mobile phone with a built-in camera. As they wander around, they take pictures of interesting objects, bizarre furniture, suits of armour or whatever else catches their eye. As well as taking photos, they'll need to remember as much as possible of what they see.

On the way home

Coming home from a family outing can be something of a let-down, with the kids – and adults – tired and often hungry.

This game provides a challenge to keep spirits up. Everyone has spent the afternoon photographing the most intriguing things they've come across. Now that the trip's over, these can be used to set the rest of the family a memory challenge.

The game starts like the traditional I Spy game which, let's be honest, most of us find rather dull. Here, though, players use the past tense and must have not only 'I spied' an object, but also photographed it.

For instance, after a visit to an old castle, a round might go: 'I spied with my little eye, something beginning with G.' The other players rack their brains for things they've spotted during the day: 'Grass?' No.

FACT BOX

In Spain, I Spy is known as **Veo, Veo** (I see, I see). In Germany, it begins **Ich sehe was, was du nicht siehst** (I see what you don't see) and in the Netherlands it's **Ik zie, ik zie, wat jij niet ziet** (with the same meaning as in German).

An interesting Italian variation is **Lupo Mangia tutto** (Wolf eats everything), in which one player is the wolf and names a starting letter: the other players have to run and touch something beginning with that letter before they're caught by the wolf.

'Graveyard?' No. 'Geese?' No. It's not until someone hits on 'Gauntlet' that they win the round – providing that the 'iSpider' can now produce a photograph of the gauntlet of a suit of armour.

How to score

The game can be played just for fun, but scoring gives it a bit more zing. Guessers get one point for a correct guess and five points if they themselves have also taken a photograph of the object. The iSpider gets two points if the others give up.

Play continues until all the photographs, or all the kids, are exhausted.

Age 5+

Lottery Bingo

3+

Players

Indoor

Recreate the passion and excitement of the Bingo Hall in your own sitting room – with only a pack of cards.

| SET UP 10 mins | PLAY TIME 20+ mins | YOU NEED a pack of cards • bingo sheets |

Bingo is a great game for all the family, as it can be played by all ages: all you have to do is listen for the number being called, and cross it off your card. But to play traditional bingo you need stacks of pre-printed cards, along with a converted hamster cage full of ping pong balls fitted with a hair dryer to spit out the numbers.

Not in the brave new world of 21st century fun and games. Here's a method that combines bingo with the great Lotto trick of allowing players to choose their own numbers. It's a far more enjoyable way to play, as it gives all the players the chance to pick their own winners.

So don't worry if you don't happen to own a hamster-cage-ball-spitting-hairdryer machine complete with numbered balls: our version needs nothing more fancy than an old pack of cards. Plus, we've devised a couple of extra twists to help keep things interesting.

Setting up

You need a selection of bingo sheets to write your numbers on. Here's one we prepared earlier:

fg-21.com/bingo.jpg

Each sheet has six bingo sets printed on it. Either download the file to your computer, or print it directly from your browser window.

There are 16 squares in each set, four for each suit. Each player choose four numbers for each suit, and writes them in the spaces under the suit symbols, as shown opposite. Rather than '1', write 'A' for the ace; and use 'J', 'Q', 'K' for Jack, Queen, King.

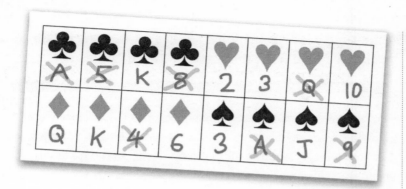

How to play

Deal a standard pack of cards between all the players (it doesn't matter if you end up with a couple of players having one more than the rest).

The youngest player starts by turning over the top card on his or her deck, and showing it to everyone. Anyone who has chosen that card can then cross it off their sheet. Play moves around the table in a clockwise direction, with each player revealing a single card, and everyone who's chosen that card crossing it off.

Two more rules

Rule 1: if a player turns over a card that they have on their own sheet, they can cross off not only that card, as normal, but any other card they like.

Rule 2: whenever a Joker is turned up, every player crosses off a card of their choosing from their sheet.

And the winner is...

The first player to cross off every card on their sheet and shout 'BINGO!' at the top of their voice.

2

Players

Indoor

Lunar Lander

Fine-tune your navigational skills with this recreation of a classic game from the dawn of the computer age.

SET UP 5 mins | **PLAY TIME 10+ mins** | **YOU NEED** a blindfold • a glass of water

In days gone by, we spent so long perfecting our skills playing Lunar Lander on arcade machines in pubs that we half-expected a NASA scout to turn up, asking if we'd be so kind as to put on spacesuits and help out on their next mission.

Our retro version can be played almost anywhere, and with whatever is to hand. We find it's a particularly good way to fill time in restaurants while waiting for the food.

Setting up

Choose an object to represent the lunar lander. A tumbler or glass is ideal, but anything that can be grasped in one hand will work fine. Next, establish the landing stage. This should be placed some distance from the landing craft, and might be a place mat, a coaster, or a piece of card. If you're in a restaurant with a paper tablecloth, simply draw on it. The older and more skilled the players, the smaller the landing zone should be.

One player is the 'pilot', the other the 'navigator'. Ideally, the pilot should be blindfolded (see page 223) but, since diners tend to look oddly at parents who blindfold their children in public, they may have to be trusted to close their eyes.

How to play

The sightless pilot operates the lunar lander with one hand, while the navigator issues verbal directions. Their shared aim is to convey the lunar module safely to the landing zone.

As in the arcade game (but presumably not in real-life lunar travel)

GOING FURTHER

If there's no glass handy, find something small lying around like a pea or piece of corn, and play using a pair of tweezers or chopsticks to grab the payload. Or try it with just a thumb and forefinger.

the commands available to the navigator are extremely limited. They are: 'right', 'left', 'forward', 'back', 'up', 'down', 'grasp' and 'release'.

Scoring

Score 5 for a perfect landing in the zone, 4 for landing mostly in it, 3 for coming down with less in than out and 1 for a safe landing anywhere else.

Make it harder

Once the simple version has been mastered, make it more complicated. Fill the glass with water so that a steady hand is needed if precious 'fuel' isn't to be spilt. Or start with the glass empty and introduce a refuelling point where the pilot must touch down and refill the module from another glass – all without looking – before setting off again for the final landing zone.

Age 8+

3+
Players

Indoor

Computer

Name that iTune

Use iTunes to play a great musical game for all the family – for free.

| SET UP 10 mins | PLAY TIME 30+ mins | YOU NEED a computer with iTunes installed |

Racing to be the first to 'name that tune' is an old favourite for all age groups. These days you don't even need to own or buy the music.

Setting up

If you don't have iTunes installed on your computer, it's easy – and free – to download and install from the Apple website. And iTunes is compatible with Windows PCs as well as Macs. You'll also need an iTunes account, though you don't need to spend any money.

Appoint a Quizmaster or Quizmasters – there can be more than one. Each Quizmaster compiles a list of tunes to be played back to the contestants. Once you get the hang of it, it takes about five minutes to complete a 10-song playlist quiz. Here's how you do it.

First, create a new playlist in iTunes ('New Playlist' from the 'File' menu). Give it an easily recognisable name.

Next, add tunes to your playlist. You could use your existing music but one great feature of iTunes is that it lets you play 30-second samples of each of the zillions of tracks in its store for free. Access the iTunes store and use the 'Search' field to find suitable music, then simply drag the tracks you want in your quiz into your playlist. There's no limit to the number of songs that can be used: it just depends how long you want each round to last.

Try to tailor your quiz to your contestants' musical tastes and knowledge: if Auntie Hester is playing, you might want to avoid Hip-Hop tracks.

TIP: *Watch out for the 'Buy song' button – unless of course you're in the mood to expand your music collection.*

How to play

Once the playlist – or playlists – have been created, the game can begin. The first Quizmaster plays each song on their playlist in turn, while the contestants compete to be the first to 'name that iTune'. Feel free to improvise buzzers. The Quizmaster should keep score, with 10 points for a correct answer and minus 10 points for a wrong one. Total up at the end of the playlist and you're ready for another round, perhaps with a new Quizmaster.

Musical themes

We recommend creating 'themed' playlists. For older players, 'TV themes' always makes for an enjoyably nostalgic contest. The iTunes store has over 150 TV theme albums ready to be ransacked, with names like *The Ultimate TV Themes Collection* and *100 TV Themes*.

For younger players, search for 'Cartoon themes' or 'Kids' party songs' (you don't really need that apostrophe, but we like to try to maintain cyber standards).

GOING FURTHER

More organised players can arrange everything in advance by uploading playlists to the iTunes store. Once you've created a playlist in iTunes, highlight it. Click on the 'Store' menu in the toolbar, and select 'Create an iMix'.

When the time comes to play the game, search for your 'iMix' playlist in the iTunes store and retrieve it onto the computer being used.

Never say die: three dice games

A trio of top-notch dice games you can play even if you've lost the dice.

SET UP 2 mins **PLAY TIME** 10+ mins **YOU NEED** a talking dice program (see page 208)

Who knows where dice go? Perhaps it's the same place as socks. We've all had the maddening experience of opening up the box of every board game in the house, only to find they've already been plundered.

Admittedly it doesn't have the same sense of theatre as shaking dice in a cup, but you can also use a computer to generate your own dice numbers. We've explained how to do this on page 208.

Here's a selection of family dice games, each requiring just one die (to use the pedant's word).

Pig

This is a simpler version of the commercial game *Pass the Pigs*.

Each player throws the dice as many times as they like, keeping track of the total of all their throws. The catch is that, as soon as they get a 1, their turn ends and they lose that round's entire score. Ideally, you want to stop just before you're about to throw a 1. But when will that be? It's a question of luck and nerve.

The first to 50 is the winner.

Bugs

Each player should have a piece of paper and something to draw with. Taking it in turns to throw, players race to construct a bug, with each number corresponding to a body part.

1 – Body
2 – Head
3 – Eye (draw one per roll)
4 – Antenna (ditto)
5 or 6 – Leg (ditto).

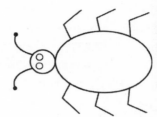

You can only start to construct your bug when you have rolled a 1 and drawn the bug's body. Similarly, you can't add eyes or antennae until you've rolled a 2 and drawn the head. The first to complete their six-legged bug is the winner.

There's no need to confine yourself to bugs: anything with discrete components will work. And with many-sided computer-generated dice available, there's no limit to the number of body parts either. For instance, why not try a dinosaur – or, if you're feeling seriously ambitious, a human skeleton?

Hundred Up

Start by making a column for each player on an A4 sheet of paper, with their name written at the top. Players then roll the dice in turn. If any get a six, they start scribbling numbers from 1 to 100 in a column below their name. Meanwhile, the other players continue to take turns to roll the dice. As soon as anyone else throws six, they grab the paper and start writing numbers up to 100 in their own column, carrying on from where they left off.

The first to get to 100 is the winner.

Age 8+

2+
Players

Indoor

Calculator

Olympic Calculators

A pentathlon of calculator games to test your digital speed and agility to the limit.

| SET UP 2 mins | PLAY TIME 15+ mins | YOU NEED a calculator • a stopwatch |

Who's the fleetest of finger in the family? These five Olympic-style races will sort the sprinters from the slow-pokes.

Ideally, each player should have a calculator but, if there aren't enough to go round, you can play with one player at a time, using a stopwatch to keep time. (Remember – all mobile phones have a stop-watch built in.)

100 metre sprint

First, each player keys in 1 ++ (the second + tells the calculator to repeat the last sum). On a 'Go!' signal, they then keep pressing the = key as fast as they can until they reach 100. The first to get there is the winner.

Hurdles

This is similar to the sprint, but every fifth pace racers have to key in a 9 rather than a 1. So the sequence goes: 1 + 1 + 1 + 1 + 9 + 1 + 1 + 1 + 1 + 9, and so on. The game continues for 10 hurdles – that is, until players have typed in the number 9 ten times. They'll need to remember to type a final = or + so that the screen displays the correct total.

Players must keep count of the number of times they press the 9 key, and may choose to do so out loud. This has the definite advantage of putting other players off their stride.

When the race is over, check the totals to make sure all players have keyed in the numbers correctly: the screen should show 130. If it's any other number, they've skipped or knocked over a hurdle and are disqualified.

Relay race

Players first key in $1 + 2 + 3 + 4 + 5 + 6 + 7 + 8 + 9$, then start from the next number ($2 + 3 + 4 + 5 + 6 + 7 + 8 + 9$), then the next ($3 + 4 + 5 + 6 + 7 + 8 + 9$) until they get to $8 + 9$, after which they just type the final 9 and press =, and they're done. The total will come to 285 if all the numbers have been keyed in correctly.

Obstacle course

In this game, the players key in the numbers 1 to 9 again, but have to hit the keys in between in the order +, ×, −, ÷. So the full sequence goes:

$$1 + 2 \times 3 - 4 \div 5 + 6 \times 7 - 8 \div 9 =$$

The answer should be 4.55 recurring. Although it's only a short sequence of numbers, it can be tricky to get the adding, multiplying, subtracting and dividing in the right order under pressure.

NOTE: *Check your calculator shows a running total after each key press. If it doesn't – and calculators on, for example, iPods don't – you'll get a different answer, because of the way they perform the operations. The solution is to press = after each operation.*

Hopscotch

This game involves athletic jumping to diagonal 'squares' on the calculator, while trying to get an accurate score.

First, players must press all the even numbers (2468) then press + to add all the odd numbers (13579), then add the even numbers, and so on – three times. This is the sum:

$$2468 + 13579 + 2468 + 13579 + 2468 + 13579$$

It takes nimble fingers to get the correct answer of 48141.

GOING FURTHER

There are dozens of variations on all these games – for example, for a 200 metre sprint players could type in $1 + 2 + 1 + 2$ and so on, until they reach 200.

Age 5+

2+

Players

Car game

On the road 1

A range of travel games to ward off those dreaded cries of 'Are we nearly there yet?'

| SET-UP 2 mins | PLAY TIME as long as you need | YOU NEED a car full of bored kids |

Here's a selection of excellent games to help pass the time and prevent squabbling. Although ideal for the car, they can also be played on train journeys or even on long family walks. Before you know it, you *are* there yet.

Country tag

The first player names a country. The next person must come up with a country beginning with that country's last letter. Depending on players' age, ability and geographical knowledge, you might allow the names of towns and cities too. So if the first player says 'Austria', the next might say 'Amsterdam', the next might chip in with 'Malawi', and so on.

The fame game

In this tag game the first player names a famous person. If it's 'David Cameron', the next player has to name someone else with the same first or last name. They might opt for 'Cameron Diaz', which could be followed by 'Cameron Crowe' and then 'Russell Crowe'.

If younger kids find it too difficult played this way, then they could instead come up with someone whose first name begins with the first letter of the previous person's surname.

Alphabet safari

Players have to spot items outside the window, beginning with successive letters of the alphabet. You might want to leave out 'Z' unless you're near a zebra farm, and you could choose to allow 'X', to stand for 'Crossing'.

Alphabet shopping

'I went to the shop and I bought an apple', says the first player. The next player must repeat that phrase, but add an object beginning with 'B': 'I went to the shop and I bought an apple and a bicycle'. Each player adds one more object until a player forgets an item in the chain. It can be made more difficult by playing with more specialised shops such as toy stores or newsagents.

The Yes/No game

One person is 'It' and the others ask them questions, trying to trip them up by getting them to say the two forbidden words, 'Yes' and 'No'. A favourite way of catching them out is to say something like 'Are you ready yet?' It takes a focused mind not to say 'yes' at this point.

Animal, vegetable, mineral

One of the most popular of all time-passing games. Somebody thinks of an object and says whether it's animal, vegetable or mineral. Everybody else has to ask questions to narrow down options until the object is finally guessed.

Good questions to ask are 'Can you eat it?', 'Do we own one?', 'Is it bigger than my head/a matchbox/this car?', 'Is it useful or ornamental?', and so on. Strictly speaking, the person thinking of the object should only answer either 'yes' or 'no', but that can make the game play clumsy: better if they just give a short response.

Many people stick to a total of 20 questions but you don't have to.

Celebrity 20 questions

This is similar to *Animal, Vegetable, Mineral*, but uses famous people, both real and fictional. Starting with the obvious 'male or female?', guessers have 20 questions to reach the correct answer.

GOING FURTHER

If you're enjoying the games so much you don't want to stop, try driving round the block a couple of times before going home. That way you'll be sure to go further.

Age 5+

2+

Players

Car game

On the road 2

More games to keep the family entertained on long journeys.

SET UP 2 mins | **PLAY TIME as long as you need** | **YOU NEED bored kids**

Still bored on that car journey? Here's a second selection of tried and tested travel games.

Pub signs

Use the three letters at the end of the number plate of the car in front as an acronym to come up with pub names. LGA could be 'Lord Gardener's Arms', for instance. These days there are all sorts of weird pub names, so it can get very surreal – if 'TBA' leads to 'The Blue Axolotl' that's fine. Short words like 'the' and 'of' may be inserted.

In a phrase

Use the four letters on number plates, the one before the numbers and three after, to come up with a phrase, which can be as silly as you like. Another variant is to make newspaper headlines (three letters work best here). In our last game 'CBM' produced 'Crushed Boy Mumbles'.

Pub cricket

Not suitable for motorways or drives through remote wildernesses, this game works best in towns or villages.

The 'batsman' scores runs based on the number of legs implied in pub names. *The White Lion*, for instance, scores four; *The King's Arms* two – the King in question almost certainly having legs as well as arms.

But the pictures on signs override the names. So if the picture on *The King's Arms* shows a lion and a unicorn, then you score eight. We've yet to see a *Centipede's Arms* sign (it can only be a matter of time).

A player is 'out' when they pass a pub that is legless.

Car cricket

Score either for cars you pass or for cars that pass you from the opposite direction, depending how busy the road is. Score 1 for a car, 2 for a motorbike, 4 for a van and 6 for anything more substantial. You're out as soon as a red car comes along, whereupon the next player goes 'in' to bat. This is good game for town and country roads, but it can be a little hard to keep up on the motorway.

Car snooker

In this game, players compile 'breaks' by spotting (rather than potting) cars in the same colour order as in snooker. So a break starts with a red car (1 point) then continues with a 'colour', then another red, then another colour, and so on. Permitted colours are: yellow (2 points), green (3 points), brown (4 points), blue (5 points), pink (6 points) and black (7 points).

Keep careful track of the break score, and as soon as a non-snooker colour, such as silver, is seen, the next player takes over.

Cast of characters

In this collaborative game, players must come up with as many characters as they can from favourite TV shows and movies, such as *The Simpsons* (with well over 100 recurring characters) or the Harry Potter movies. If you run out of ideas for TV and film characters, any other category of person or thing will also work – how about objects in the night sky, for example?

The world will always need new car games. Share yours online.

fg-21.com/forum

From the archives...

Consequences

A diverting game of nonsensical narrative.

Three players upwards write at the top of a piece of paper the name of a man – famous, fictional or a friend. The paper is folded down so that just that name is concealed, then passed to the left.

Players now write 'met' then a woman's name, and again fold and pass the paper left. They continue by writing 'at' and a place where they met; 'He said to her...', plus a suitable phrase; 'She said to him...', with whatever she said; 'They then...', explaining what they did; and finally, 'And the consequence was...', with the denouement.

The players now pass their sheets to the left once more, and each unfolds and reads out the full story before them.

Penny football

Football as it has been played at schools for generations.

Make two goals at opposite ends of a table. Players take it in turns to flick a two-pence piece 'player' to hit the 'ball', which is a penny. They get up to three flicks per turn and are not permitted to score directly from a kick-off in the centre of the playing area. If a player misses the ball, it becomes their opponent's turn.

Coin snatching

Flip a coin off your elbow and catch it.

Bend your arm back and place a 10p coin on your elbow. Flip your arm forwards and try to catch the coin in one motion with your hand, palm-down. It takes some doing.

Once you've mastered that, try two coins. And then three. And then four. But you may have trouble matching the world record, which currently stands at a perfect catch of 100 coins in one go.

Fig 1: The coin balanced on the elbow.

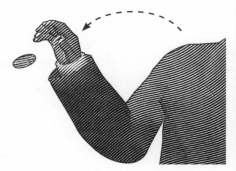

Fig 2: Catching the coin.

Racing demons

The boisterous card game
for 3 or more players

Each player has a different pack of cards and deals themselves 12 face down with a 13th face up on top. This is the 'croupette'. They then deal four cards face up in a line beside their croupette, keeping the rest in their hand.

At the word 'Go' players move any face-up aces to the middle, replacing them from the top of their croupette and turning over the croupette's next card. Each player always has five face-up cards: the top of the croupette and four beside it.

Players go through their remaining cards as fast as possible, three at a time, building up any suits in the middle from ace upwards. They can play on any piles, not just those they start. Any aces go into the middle. Players must watch for chances to move face-up cards to a pile of that suit in the centre (replacing them from the top of their croupette). If no-one can play, all players move their top card to the bottom before resuming counting in threes. Anyone placing the final King onto a middle suit takes that pile.

The first to play their final croupette card (not the four by it) calls 'Stop'.

The finishing player gets 10 points. Players get 5 points for each pile completed with a King. All players lose a point for each card not yet played, and gain one for every card played into the middle.

Wooden spoon race

A tournament involving unusual
contortions among party guests.

This is similar to passing the orange under your neck, but does not require untoward intimacy. You need two wooden spoons to which a long piece of string can be securely tied, either through a hole or to a notch in the handle.

Arrange everyone into two teams. At the world 'Go', the player with the spoon must pass it down one arm and one leg of their clothing and then pass it to the next player. The first team to get the spoon through the clothing of all players wins.

Think of a number

One player thinks of a number
and the others must guess it.

The first player thinks of a number between 1 and 100. The other players then take it in turns to guess the number. After each guess, the first player may say only 'too high' or 'too low'. The winner is the one who guesses the correct number first.

1+

Players

Indoor

Computer

Online games: six of the best

Our favourite half-dozen online games that the whole family can play.

SET UP 2 mins | PLAY TIME 10 mins to 3 hrs | YOU NEED computer with internet

Escape the room

Figure out clues and find your way out of the room. A great co-operative pastime for older kids, or younger kids and a parent. This will have you puzzling for hours: **fg-21.com/escape**

Continuity

Your goal is to get the stick man to the exit. You do this by moving the rooms around using the arrow keys. The games start easy, but get progressively harder: **fg-21.com/continuity**

Toss the penguin

One of the oddest games we've come across, Pingu Throw is great fun and simple to learn. Your goal is to whack the falling penguin so it flies as far as possible: **fg-21.com/penguin**

Where in the world

You're shown a series of photographs, and have to guess where in the world they were taken. The game is played on Picasa, Google's photo sharing service: **fg-21.com/where**

Fancypants

A running, jumping, dodging the spiders game that's easy to pick up, very stylish to look at and great fun – the perfect web game for kids of all ages: **fg-21.com/fancy**

Augmented reality

Not a game, but an idea of what the future of interactive computing might look like. Print out the special sheet, hold it up to a webcam, and a moving 3D model pops out of the screen to appear in front of you. It's an amazing preview of the way we might routinely interact with our computers in the not-so-distant future: **fg-21.com/reality**

GOING FURTHER

If you enjoyed the Escape the Room game, you'll find a lot more in a similar vein at **fg-21.com/escape2**. They're not all as slick as the one shown here, but they are great fun to figure out.

And for more augmented reality experiences, check out **fg-21.com/reality2**

There are many fantastic online games – share your favourites.

fg-21.com/forum

Age 5+

5+

Players

Indoor

Party game

Out of control air traffic

A game of nerve and skill where a controller guides human planes to their landing strip without crashing.

| SET UP 10 mins | PLAY TIME 20+ mins | YOU NEED coloured hats • matching cushions |

The job of an air traffic controller is not an easy one. They have to direct a large number of planes through crowded airspace without fatal crashes. Our game allows you to recreate the challenge of the real thing without quite the same degree of stress, using a handful of players, an open space and some brightly coloured clothing.

Setting up

One player is the Controller, and the rest are the Planes. Each Plane should wear a hat (or a scarf or jumper) of a different colour, to enable the air traffic controller to identify them easily. Of course, they could simply be referred to by name, but using colours makes the process seem more technical – and has the added difficulty that each Plane has to remember which colour hat he or she is wearing.

Near the centre of the large room or, better, outdoor space, place a cushion, coat, rug or sheet of paper the same colour as each of the hats, and arrange them as in the diagram opposite. These are the landing strips, to which each Plane must be guided by the Controller.

Next, position each Plane on the perimeter of the playing area at the other side from their target strip, as shown on the facing page.

How to play

At a signal from the Controller, all the Planes start walking towards the centre. They should walk slowly, heel-to-toe fashion.

The task of the Controller is now to guide all the Planes to their colour-coded landing strip, without crashing into each other. To this end, the Controller must issue directions, by saying first the colour of

72

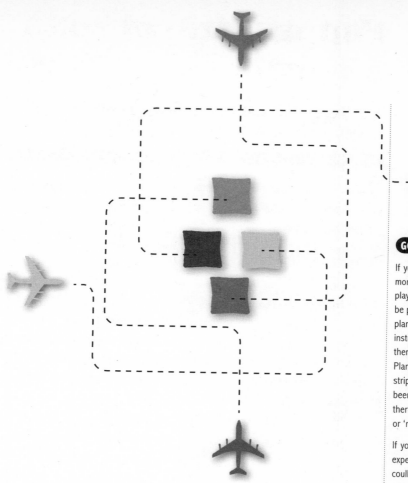

GOING FURTHER

If your group has more than five players, the game can be played with more planes. A further instruction should then be used to get Planes off the landing strip, once they have been safely 'stopped' there. Perhaps 'taxi' or 'refuel'?

If you feel like experimenting, you coulld even try adding a second Controller, being sure to allocate planes clearly between the two.

the Plane, then either 'left' or 'right'. No other commands are allowed until the Planes have reached their landing strip, at which point they must be told to 'stop'. The Planes should try to respond correctly to the instructions, turning 90 degrees with each 'left' or 'right' command – but if they make a mistake, it's up to the Controller to rectify it, as in real life.

The Controller's task will involve directing the Planes to perform complicated manoeuvres around each other. Once all Planes have either crashed or been guided safely to their landing strips, the game ends and another player can take a turn at being the Controller.

Papparazzi pursuits

3+
Players

Outdoor

Active

Mobile phone

Hone your stalking skills with these photographic variations of hide and seek.

SET UP 10 mins | **PLAY TIME 1+ hr** | **YOU NEED** a camera or phone for each player

Adults may like long walks, but kids are often less excited by the prospect. Here are two games, based on the exploits of papparazzi photographers, that will help them forget they're doing wholesome exercise.

Papparazzi nametag

Each player needs to be equipped with a digital camera (a camera phone will work fine), and should have a nametag – a piece of paper with their name written on it – pinned to their backs.

The aim is to photograph the other players' nametags as many times as possible, while trying to avoid being snapped yourself. The winner is the player with the highest number of legible photos of other players' names at the end of the game.

Rather than being played for a set time, this game can last throughout a walk, with the children haring off into undergrowth, hiding behind trees and so on, while you enjoy the scenery in peace. Unless, that is, you want to join in too.

Papparazzi bounty hunters

In this game, which can be played on any family outing, the papparazzi must snap the other members of the family in five pre-selected poses. As a starting suggestion, try these:

- Pointing
- Laughing
- Picking their nose
- Looking silly
- Looking good

With five categories and four other family members, that makes a total of 20 possible photos. At the end of the day, look through all the snaps and tot up the scores. As well as livening up any day out, this game is a great way of making sure you have interesting photos of your family – even if some of them won't be particularly flattering.

GOING FURTHER

Take the lack of a set time frame to extremes by playing this game over the course of a holiday, or even a whole year.

All ages

Pass the parsnip

5+

Players

Indoor

Party game

Mobile phone

The 21st-century version of Pass the Parcel, without wasting all that wrapping paper.

SET UP 10 mins | **PLAY TIME 15+ mins** | **YOU NEED** two mobile phones • a parsnip

In our environmentally friendly take on the party classic, players pass round a phone instead of a heavily wrapped parcel, with periodic text messages announcing the prizes – or forfeits.

Unlike Pass the Parcel, our version can be enjoyed by players of any age: simply adapt the forfeits and prizes accordingly.

Setting up

Prepare a selection of special prizes, along with some party bag treats, then write out a list of suitable forfeits. For younger players, they might be:

- Pull a funny face
- Do a somersault
- Hop around on one leg
- Act like a monkey, dog or chicken
- Say 'I am a green tomato' without laughing

And, for older players, this sort of thing:

- Tell a joke
- Say 'truly rural' 5 times
- Impersonate Homer Simpson singing in the shower
- Whistle the National Anthem
- Dance like your dad

For older players, you can also use quiz-style questions: name six makes of car or five famous Frenchmen for example. A wrong answer naturally results in a forfeit.

Preparing the phones

Photograph a parsnip (or download a picture of one) and set it to be the desktop image on a phone. This is the phone to be passed around by the players.

If possible, co-opt another 'controller' or two. Each controller should have a phone programmed with the parsnip phone's number.

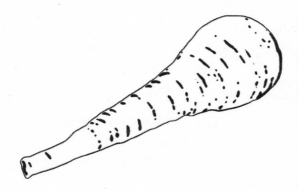

How to play

As the players pass the 'parsnip' around, the controllers take it in turns to text forfeits or questions to it, interspersed with the word 'PRIZE' as many times as there are special prizes.

Having more than one controller helps keep the gaps between texts short, but a moderately quick-fingered individual will manage fine. (See page 108 for a game to boost your texting speed.)

The player holding the phone when a text is received must enact the forfeit – or, if they receive a 'PRIZE' message, they collect a special prize from the Controller. If the phone receives a call or message from an external source during the game, all players get a prize.

After all the special prizes have been won, text 'GAME OVER' and give a parsnip to whoever is left holding the phone.

HELP THE OED

The Oxford English Dictionary is the ultimate authority on English usage. As well as providing definitions of every word in the language, it also cites the first known use of the word or phrase in print.

But there are some gaps in their knowledge. Here's a striking one: they can't find any printed reference to Pass the Parcel earlier than 1967. So if you, or your parents, or your grandparents, played this game before that date, and wrote to someone about it, drop the OED a line!

Phone phrenzy

All ages

4+

Players

Indoor/Outdoor

Party game

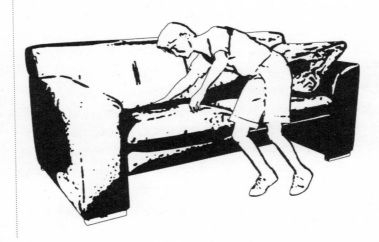

Mobile phone

Find the phone. It's calling you – but can you tell where it's hiding?

SET UP 10 mins | **PLAY TIME 15+ mins** | **YOU NEED** two mobile phones

What do you do when you can't find your mobile? Call it, of course, praying it isn't set to silent mode. Yet even when it rings, it can be surprisingly hard to tell where it is, leaving you to dash about, trying desperately to work out where the noise is coming from before it cuts to voicemail. We've put those hours of frustration to good use in this new game.

Setting up

The controller hides a mobile phone somewhere in the house or the garden – under a cushion, upstairs in the bathroom, or stuffed into a bush – taking care not to be observed. For outside hiding places, a thin plastic bag should be used to protect the phone from getting wet. The controller also hides a prize, in a different place from the phone.

How to play

Assemble all the hunters. If you're playing indoors, they should be in a different room from the phone; or, if you're outside, in a different part of the garden.

Call the phone, allowing it to ring only once or twice before hanging up. With only a very rough idea of where to look, the players will head off in what they think is the right direction. Keep calling from time to time, and they'll begin to zero in on the secret hiding place. When enough of them are close by, leave them to hunt for it as if it were an old-fashioned thimble.

The person who finds the phone should then call the controller – there will be umpteen missed calls from the number – to be told where to pick up their prize.

The three-phone version

Instead of just one, hide two phones some distance apart. This way, you can tease the hunters. As soon as they're going in one direction, taunt them by ringing the other phone. Who will be tempted away to look for that, and who will stick around to concentrate on finding the first one?

A personal touch

Record your own voice on the hidden phone and make it the ring-tone. How much more frustrating if the hunters hear a voice calling out 'Here I am!' as they search! When they start to get close, you can ring off after it's said the single word 'Here'.

GOING FURTHER

Instead of having the person who finds the phone call the controller to find out where to get their prize, the controller could send a text message with the reward's location.

Age 11+

2+
Players

Indoor

Computer

Racing with Google Maps

Race around the country on real roads using Google Maps and Google Street View.

SET UP 2+ mins | **PLAY TIME 10+ mins** | **YOU NEED** a computer with internet access

Google Maps is a very practical route-finding application, but it's also a great source of fun. Here are two games to get you started. With two or more computers, you can race against your friends in real time.

The Street View challenge

Go into *maps.google.co.uk* and search for the Houses of Parliament. Switch into Google Street View (see page 218). Your task: to 'drive' from here to Harrods, in Knightsbridge, as fast as you can.

Click anywhere within the Street View to advance. With each click, you'll jump forwards and you'll see a new view from that position. It helps if you have a knowledge of the local geography; otherwise, use the Directions facility to work out the fastest route.

London to Leeds on the M1

This game uses a Map view of the country. Enter 'Brent Cross London' in the search field, which will take you to the start of the M1 motorway. The motorway is helpfully marked in bright blue, making it easy to pick out as you race across the landscape.

The game is to follow the M1 all the way to Leeds, but here's the difficult part: you move, not by using the mouse or the trackpad, but with the arrow keys on your keyboard.

When you press the keys, the map will scroll slowly at first, picking up speed the longer you hold down the keys. You can press more than one key at once, so pressing Up and Left will make the map scroll in a North-Westerly direction. But, just like in a real car, if you're going too fast it's easy to spin off the road: the trick is to go just quickly enough so that you can keep the motorway on screen at all times.

NOTE: *For a fair race, all players need to be 'zoomed in' to the same level.*

GOING FURTHER

The start and end locations we've given here are just suggestions, of course. Pick a route in your local neighbourhood, perhaps starting at your house and finishing at a grandparent's house or a local attraction.

You don't need to stick to motorways in the second game, either, although their bright blue colouring does make them easier to follow.

Found a great racing route? See how others fare with it.

fg-21.com/forum

Remote control football

Guide a football through a door with a remote control car – while blindfolded.

SET UP 2 mins | PLAY TIME 15+ mins | YOU NEED remote control car • football

Remote control cars, robots, Daleks and the like are the sort of toys for which the initial enthusiasm often dies down. But this game's a good reason for getting their batteries charged up again.

Driving lessons

Before the game proper, players should practise their blindfold driving skills. One person is the Controller, the other the Director. The Controller holds the remote control, and is blindfolded (see page 223). The Director – sighted – has to guide them.

You need a decent-sized room with a clear floor space, not too cluttered by furniture and other awkward obstacles. Set out a simple

course and get the Controller to navigate around it to the Director's instructions, which should be in the form 'forward', 'back', 'left', 'right' and 'stop'.

Bring on the ball

Once the Controller has mastered blindfolded driving, introduce a lightweight football or, if the remote control vehicle is small, a tennis ball. The aim of the game is for the Controller to use the car to steer the ball out of the door, even though they can't see either the door or the car.

Once the ball has successfully been nudged out of the room, the two players can change roles, or other players can be drafted in to take their place.

For a competitive version, time how long it takes each person to get the ball out of the room from the same spot.

Robot politician

2+

Use your computer's ability to talk as a way of creating hilariously robotic conversations.

| SET UP 10 mins | PLAY TIME 15+ mins | YOU NEED two computers |

Everyone's sick of hearing politicians spouting pre-prepared phrases that bear no connection to the question they're being asked. We've taken that to extremes with a set of questions and answers that are *both* set up in advance.

In our game we get our computers to read the phrases out for us, rather than saying them ourselves. The robotic voice simply adds to the fun and incongruity.

Setting up

Each player has a laptop or desktop computer, running a word processing program with 'Text-to-Speech' enabled (it's easy: see page 224 for guidance). One player is the interviewee, the other is the interviewer. A topic for the interview is chosen (for instance, MPs' expenses), then each player takes five minutes to type as many possible questions or answers, depending on their role.

TIP: *We've found it helps the game if a list of general 'filler' phrases for any situation is prepared before the five-minute countdown starts. Some ideas are: 'Yes', 'No', 'What do you mean?', 'How dare you!', 'I'm afraid I don't quite understand', 'I've never been so insulted in my life', and so on. Of course, these can then be saved and re-used next time the game is played.*

How to play

Once all the phrases have been typed in, the interviewer begins by highlighting a question from the list, and makes the computer speak that phrase.

The politician then chooses from his or her pre-prepared list the phrase that best answers (or perhaps evades) the question that has been asked. The interviewer can ask questions in any order, and the politician doesn't have to use all the answers on the list: the same answer can be given multiple times, if it matches the question. The aim is to keep the conversation going for as long as possible.

GOING FURTHER

Extra fun can be had by playing around with your system's 'Text-to-Speech' settings. Both Windows and Mac operating systems allow you to choose different speaking 'characters'. On our Mac, for instance, we have 'Bruce', 'Fred', 'Agnes' and 'Kathy', as well as 'Princess' and the very aptly named 'Deranged'. There is also the option to vary the speed.

Some sample questions

Did you or did you not spend taxpayers' money on stocking your fishpond with carp?

Why should anyone vote for you?

Why should we believe anything you say?

Do you have a message for your constituents?

Are you going to answer my last question?

Are you going to apologise?

Some sample answers

The whole incident has been regrettable, and I regret that it has happened.

No comment.

Last month I went on a fact-finding trip to Barbados.

I'd send them all to prison if I had the chance.

I'm afraid I can't tell you that.

I will, if you'll just let me finish.

Of course, you don't have to stick with slimy politicians and Paxman-style interviewers. Some other situations you might try are:

● A teacher asking a student why he hasn't handed in his homework.

● A door-to-door salesman tying to sell miniature umbrellas.

● A parent asking a teenage child why they came home at 4am when the curfew was midnight.

● Chatting someone up in a very loud nightclub.

There's no limit to the possibilities. You'll be amazed how long you can make the exchanges last – and how funny it is to hear two computers deep in conversation.

Which situations have you had most fun with? Tell others on the F&G forum.

fg-21.com/forum

85

Age 8+

2-4
Players

Indoor

Mobile phone

Rock, paper, pixels

Rock, paper, scissors – the 21st-century way.

SET UP 5+ mins | PLAY TIME 10+ mins | YOU NEED mobile phone • things to photograph

Rock beats scissors, paper beats rock, and scissors beats paper: everyone knows how to play this old game. It was invented in Japan in the 19th century, and then spread everywhere else. And yet, despite its venerable age, it is still being played using those oh-so-old-fashioned hand gestures. It doesn't have to be: here's a way to bring it more up to date.

Setting up

The players go off with their phones to take three pictures representing the three outcomes. Scissors will probably always have to be scissors, but 'rocks' and 'paper' could be conveyed in a variety of ways – and part of the enjoyment is coming up with fresh ideas.

How to play: the standard version

The players ready their phones so they can select one of the three pictures they've just snapped. Keeping the screen hidden, they bring up their chosen photo. After chanting 'one, two, three', they each thrust their phones forward, comparing the images to see who's won.

How to play: the live version

Place a rock, a piece of paper and a pair of scissors in close proximity to one another on a table. On the count of three, each player takes a picture of one of the objects, doing their best to conceal what they are snapping from their opponents. This is easier if the camera is set to maximum zoom, allowing the photo to be taken from a distance. On a second count of three, all players reveal what's on their screens.

How to play: the bluffers' version

This version can only be played with two players and brings a new element of bluffing to the traditional game.

Using either of the playing styles above (i.e. 'standard' or 'live'), both players bring up one of the three items on their screen. But instead of showing their opponent, they then place their phone face down on the table.

The first player then *says* one of 'rock', 'paper' or 'scissors'. This should not be a bluff, but what is actually on their screen.

The second player responds, also saying one of the three objects, but with this difference – they are allowed to bluff. So if the first player says 'paper' and the second player has a losing rock on their screen, they may choose to say 'scissors' instead of coming clean. Obviously, if the second player already has a winning picture, there will be no need to bluff. Beware excessive bluffing: if your rival calls it correctly they get extra points (see below).

The first player must then decide whether to believe the second player or to 'call their bluff'. If the former, players simply pick up their phones without showing the screens, and another round begins, with roles reversed. If the latter, the phones are flipped over and the truth revealed.

Score one point for a normal victory, five points for correctly calling a bluff, minus 5 points for incorrectly calling a bluff.

GOING FURTHER

In **Old Lady, Assassin, Businessman**, the old lady trounces the assassin by hitting him with her cane, the assassin shoots the businessman and the businessman takes care of the old lady by putting her in an old people's home. Unless you live in a very unusual household, you'll have to think laterally to find photographs for this one. Perhaps a teapot, a toy gun and a briefcase?

We also love the **Cat, Microwave, Tinfoil** variation, though this might not be suitable for younger, more sensitive children, for obvious reasons. Cat beats foil by tearing it to pieces, tinfoil beats microwave by setting it on fire and microwave beats the cat by cooking it. And no, do not try it at home.

Age 11+

1+

Players

Outdoor

GPS device

Satellite shenanigans

A roundup of some of the many GPS-based games that are fun to play and get the family out of doors.

SET UP 15+ mins | **PLAY TIME 2+ hrs** | **YOU NEED** a GPS device or SatNav

As well as geocaching (see page 28), there is a growing range of other games that can be played if you have a GPS or GPS-equipped phone. Even without one, you can still participate in some of these, like waymarking, benchmarking and trigpointing.

Geodashing

Teams of up to five players have to find and visit as many 'dashpoints' or 'waypoints' as they can within a time limit. These are randomly selected all over the world by computer, so there are bound to be some near you.

Unlike geocaching, there is nothing physical to see at a dashpoint. Get within 100 metres and you score a find, providing you can describe it in detail or post a photo. The playing field is the entire planet.

Each game lasts a month. Details at *geodashing.gpsgames.org*.

Geodashing golf

'Golfers' use their GPS devices to get to 18 random spots. The closer they get, the lower the score, playing on their own or against others. Shorter games of 9 holes can be played on foot or bicycle. You play at *golf.gpsgames.org*.

Waymarking

People who come across interesting places or objects take photos, mark them using their GPS and then post details of their 'waymark' online at *waymarking.com*. There are over a quarter of a million waymarks worldwide in almost 1,000 different categories. As with elementary geocaching, you don't actually have to have a GPS unit to participate, particularly as waymarks aren't hidden.

Look up the waymarks in an area you're visiting for the first time or see if there are some intriguing sights in an area you thought you knew well. Your nearest waymarks might include old milestones, historical relics like limestone kilns, civil war battlefields, or just picturesque spots. Found something interesting? Upload it yourself.

Benchmarking and trigpointing

Benchmarks and trig points were used in the past by map-makers. You can find their locations online and then visit them with or without the assistance of a GPS.

Find out more at *bench-marks.org.uk* and *trigpointinguk.com*.

GPS drawing

Some artists download the tracks of journeys they have taken from GPS devices and use it as the basis for pictures, sculptures or animation. By walking around Port Meadow in Oxford, for instance, one artist created a giant virtual spider. Another made a vast elephant by driving around the streets of Brighton. It's like a giant etch-a-sketch. See it at *gpsdrawing.com*.

If you'd like to try this yourself, use the free online tool GPS Visualizer at *gpsvisualizer.com*, which has a freehand drawing tool linked to a world map (great for geography homework). It can also do many useful things with GPS data, such as creating maps and geocoding addresses, coming up with suggestions for round trips, as well as telling you the shortest way to get from one point to another. And if you want to know the exact distance between two locations, this is the place to go.

GOING FURTHER

Some GPS games are held as events taking place on just one day so keep your eyes open online for news of any interesting ones coming up.

Share your drawings and waymarks with others online via the forum.

fg-21.com/forum

From the archives...

Marbles

A tournament involving skill and dexterity with spherical glass balls.

Among many variations of this hallowed game, the most common is Ringo or Ring Taw. A chalk circle is inscribed on the ground, no larger than 10 feet across. A number of marbles, which should be smaller than the players' own striking marbles (their 'shooters') are placed in the centre.

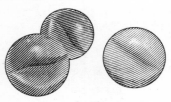

From the perimeter, players use their shooter to knock marbles out of the ring while keeping their shooter within its circumference. Any marbles bumped from the circle are kept and that player continues from where his shooter lies. If their shooter leaves the ring or they fail to knock any marbles out of it, play passes to their rival.

Should a player succeed in knocking his opponent's shooter from the ring, while their own shooter remains in it, victory is theirs and they may confiscate the marbles their opponent has won.

Note: Players should refrain from playing this with the Elgin Marbles, for fear of provoking a diplomatic incident.

Picturequences

A pictorial adaptation of the game of Chinese Whispers.

Each player begins by writing a bizarre sentence at the top of a sheet of paper. These are passed to the left and players must now try to convey the sentence in a drawing. The sheet is then folded to cover the words, and again passed to the left.

The next player writes a sentence to explain what they think is happening in the picture, which is likely to be of an outlandish nature. They then fold the sheet so only the words can be seen and pass it on. The game continues for several rounds, concluding with a sentence. The sheets of paper are then all unfolded and the first sentences compared with the last.

Potato croquet

An exceedingly droll contest utilising discarded hosiery.

Put a couple of potatoes or apples into one leg of a pair of unwanted tights, tying the other around the player's waist; the weighted part should almost but not quite reach the floor. The player must move a balloon about a course or try to hit it into a goal solely by swinging the 'bat'.

Two players can play a version of football against each other. This may also serve as a relay game for parties.

Who am I?

*A diversion involving identity-
solving conundrums.*

With this party game, the Post-It Note finds its true métier. The names of famous people, real or fictional, are written down and stuck to guests' foreheads as they arrive, so that they can't read them themselves.

Players must wander around, asking questions in an attempt to find out who they are. They should only receive 'yes' or 'no' answers, however. Of course, all the other guests will be able to see who they are – just as they themselves can see the identities of the other guests.

An interesting variation is to require partygoers to treat other guests as if they actually are the celebrity in question. This can be an amusing and entertaining way for guests to ascertain the name on their foreheads.

Izzy's dizzy

*An active party game for
children of all ages.*

Popular with scouts and guides, this needs two teams of three or more and a couple of mops or broomsticks whose handles have smooth ends. If the handle can be removed, so much the better. Avoid handles where splinters seem likely.

The first player in each team runs to their stick, places it upright with their forehead resting on it and runs around it 10 times, their team counting the turns.

When done, they must overcome their giddiness, run back to their team and touch the next person who does the same. The first team to finish is the winner.

Shop swap

Age 8+

2+

Players

Outdoor

Kill boredom at airports or shopping centres by creatively adapting signs with Scrabble letters.

| SET UP 5 mins | PLAY TIME 20+ mins | YOU NEED digital camera • Scrabble letters |

These days virtually every mobile phone can take pictures of surprisingly good quality. Using them with Scrabble letters to alter the words around us is a great way of staving off tedium. The game is particularly suitable for occasions when you're somewhere with lots of shops and time to kill.

How to play

You need a bag of Scrabble letters. Family members – either singly or together – must then hunt for amusing ways to change the lettering of signs, posters, product labels etc, using one or two letters held up in front of the camera.

Creative

Digital camera

So, for instance, House of Fraser might become Mouse of Fraser. A 'changing room' might become a 'changing roof' or, with the use of an 'H' across the first two letters, a 'hanging room'. The 'lighting' department could become the 'fighting' department or even, if the sign is large and the player dextrous, the 'licking' department.

Examine everyone's efforts when you're all together later. If you want to score, give a point for each photo taken, five for any that are unique and 10 for a photo that raises a laugh from another family member.

Here are a few suggestions to get you started...

Original name	**New name**
Topshop	**M**opshop, Topsh**I**p, To**Y**shop
Boots	**H**oots, Boo**Z**e
Currys	**F**urrys, **SL**urrys, **W**urrys
French Connection	**B**ench Connection, **W**ench Connection
Habitat	**S**Habitat, **FL**abitat
Early Learning Centre	**N**early Learning Centre
Dorothy Perkins	Dorothy **GH**erkins
Sony	**B**ony
O2	**C**O$_2$
Staples	Sta**B**les
Post Office	**L**ost Office (as well as one of our favourites, **GH**ost Office)
Topman	To**Y**man, T**A**pman.

PARENTS NOTE: *Naughtiness does have a habit of creeping into this game, so be prepared to use your acting skills to stay po-faced if the kids display a wider familiarity with the vernacular than you were expecting.*

Age 8+

6+

Players

Indoor

Stopwatch/timer

Shopping channel charades

A hilarious new game where you're a TV salesmen and your team mates try to guess what you're selling.

| SET UP 5 mins | PLAY TIME 30+ mins | YOU NEED pens and paper • phone or stopwatch |

TV shopping channel sales people are the modern equivalent of those demonstrators who haunted old-style department stores, trying to persuade people to buy bizarre gadgets unavailable anywhere else, and which usually spent the rest of their life rusting away in a cupboard.

Who suspected that these demonstrators would get their own TV stations, where they continue to exercise their powers of persuasion to part us with our hard-earned cash? But much as we mock those TV hucksters, their job is far harder than it looks – as the players of this game will find out.

Setting up

Split into two equal teams. Each team must come up with a variety of objects for the members of the other team to 'sell' to each other. They can be anything, as long as they exist in reality. So a hovercraft is allowed; a time machine is not.

TV demonstrators rarely call a spade a spade. And neither can players in this game. They must not mention the name of the object. To make things trickier still, the teams write down three further forbidden words for each item. So, for instance, if the object is 'pencil', the demonstrator may be forbidden not only to say the word 'pencil', but also 'pen', 'write' and 'lead'.

So for each object, the team must write down:

- The object to be sold
- Three words that must not be spoken when selling the object

How to play

Teams take it in turn. At the start of each round, one team passes details of the object to be sold, together with the three forbidden words, to the opposition's 'demonstrator' player.

Without miming or using helpful gestures, the demonstrator must then talk about the object as if they're selling it on a TV shopping channel. The aim is to get their teammates to guess what it is as quickly as possible.

The other team holds the stopwatch, and at the start of the sales pitch sets it to count down one minute. If the object is guessed, the score is the number of seconds remaining – this represents the price at which the item is sold. If the object isn't guessed, there is no score.

During the demonstrator's spiel, the other team should check no untoward gestures are being used. If they are, they can order the demonstrator to put their hands behind their back. A truly heinous infraction means they are disqualified for that round.

'Hat' variation

The demonstrator is given a hat containing multiple pieces of paper, with each displaying one object he or she must hawk, along with its associated forbidden words. He or she begins by picking one piece out and trying to sell it, moving on to the next as soon as it is guessed.

The countdown timer is in operation as before, but the sales pitch continues for the full minute, with 100 points (or pounds, or dollars or yen) being notched up per item sold.

GOING FURTHER

You can make things more fiendish (and funnier) by getting demonstrators to assume foreign accents as they try to sell their wares. Or make them do their pitch in a coded language like 'eggy peggy'.

Sixty-three beans

A 'Countdown' style numbers game with a modern twist, where the Quizmaster gets to pose as a maths genius.

We tend to think of telephone numbers as comprising only digits. But almost all telephone keypads, not just those on text-equipped mobile phones, have letters on the keys as well as numbers.

2	3	4	5	6	7	8	9
ABC	DEF	GHI	JKL	MNO	PQRS	TUV	WXYZ

This is a hangover from the old days, when Britain's telephone exchanges used to have names. The most famous number of all was Scotland Yard, which you'd reach by asking the operator for 'Whitehall 1212'. But enough history; here's the game.

FUN AND GAMES

1	2 ABC	3 DEF
4 GHI	5 JKL	6 MNO
7 PQRS	8 TUV	9 WXYZ
*	0	#

The game

In the popular television series *Countdown,* players are given a random selection of numbers, and have to add, subtract, multiply and divide them to get as close as they can to a target final result.

In our version, the numbers are not chosen at random, but selected by the Quizmaster – who then gets to play the role immortalised by 'Carol Vorderman' and appear to be a maths wizard.

Setting up

Each player needs a mobile phone, or a diagram of a mobile phone keypad such as the one on the previous page. You can download a printable version here:

fg-21.com/mobile

The printout has two 'mobiles' on each sheet, so you can slice them down the middle and give one to each of two players.

How to play

The Quizmaster comes up with a common word, such as 'beans'. He or she then uses the phone keypad to 'spell out' the word in numbers – in the case of 'beans' the numbers are 2, 3, 2, 6 and 7. The Quizmaster now adds, subtracts, multiplies or divides those numbers in any way they like, making sure all the numbers are used, but each one only once. So they might go for 2 + 3 + 6 − 2 × 7, which equals 63. Finally they announce the challenge to the other players thus: '63 beans'.

Racing against the clock, the contestants now take the word 'beans' and convert back it into numbers, using the phone keypad. They then get as close they can to 63 by adding, subtracting, multiplying or dividing all of those numbers, in any combination they choose. They have 60 seconds to complete the calculation, and whoever gets closest wins. Ideally the countdown should be measured on a stopwatch or a mobile phone, with a suitably dramatic or bizarre noise being set as the signal for 'time up'.

The great thing about this game is that it makes the Quizmaster look like a genius, since he or she is always able to demonstrate a solution at the end of the round, having had to work it out in advance in order to set the puzzle in the first place.

2+

Skyping Scaramouche!

Three great new games to play face to face – even if you're at opposite ends of the earth.

SET UP 10 mins | **PLAY TIME 15+ mins** | **YOU NEED** two computers with webcams

Video chat systems like Skype, Windows Live Messenger and Mac's iChat were, until recently, the stuff of science fiction. Now anyone with a computer can not only talk to a friend or relative anywhere in the world but also see them – for free. You can also play some great games.

The three below require two computers with webcams. Both players must be signed into a video chat service. Of course, it isn't compulsory to be separated by a vast distance: they're just as fun when played from two different rooms of the same house.

Kim's game

This game, first described in Rudyard Kipling's novel *Kim*, was originally a method of training spies to be observant. A taskmaster presented a tray of jewels, then surreptitiously removed one. The trainee spy had to describe the missing jewel.

In our version, each player first arranges a series of objects behind them, such as books, games, toys, ornaments, table lamps, and so on.

The players have a minute to study the other's room. They then each cover up their own webcam by draping a sock or handkerchief over it, and remove a single object.

When both are ready (remember they can still talk to each other), they simultaneously take off the 'blindfolds' and try to spot what has been taken away. The first to get it right scores a point, whereupon the cameras are covered again and another pair of objects is taken away. If neither gets it right within a minute, the next round begins.

Of course, this game only works if each player sits to one side to allow the other a view of the room!

What's that noise?

In this game, each player gathers a selection of household objects that make a noise. The players take it in turns to make that noise, off camera, and then challenge the other player to guess what it is.

These are the sort of objects you might choose:

- a pair of scissors
- a couple of spoons to be banged together
- a glass of water into which coins can be dropped
- a rubber band stretched tight and twanged.

For more suggestions for noisy household objects, see the Sound Effects game (page 186).

The security guard's conundrum

Here one player is a security guard and sits monitoring the scene in the other's room, where several players, whose identity is already known to the guard, lurk off camera. One of these – the 'thief' – puts on clothing belonging to an accomplice and conceals their whole head with a mask. Then, in full view of the webcam, the thief blatantly 'steals' something from the room.

The players again jumble up their clothing before reappearing to take part in a police-style identity lineup. The security guard must now guess which one committed the theft.

ON THE MOVE

If you have a recent iPhone or iPod Touch, you can make use of the new FaceTime feature, which allows video chat – for free – over a wifi network. Even if you're only playing at home, try hiding in an unusual spot and getting your co-FaceTimer to work out where you are!

Age 8+

2
Players

Indoor

Active

Snakes alive

Race to lay out a snake of cards as another player directs you which way to turn.

SET UP 5 mins | PLAY TIME 5+ mins | YOU NEED a pack of playing cards

A classic retro computer game, *Snake* got a new breath of life with the arrival of early mobile phones. We've come up with two versions that need nothing more high-tech than a pack of cards.

How to play: 21st century classic version

The playing area can be any flat surface with clearly defined boundaries: a large table or the floor will both do fine. Place some obstacles around the area – cushions, toys, books and mugs will all do the trick – and you're ready to begin.

The concept is simple. One player is the Snake, who places the cards; the other is the Operator, who controls the Snake's direction. The Snake begins by laying a single card in the middle of the room, then keeps laying down cards in a straight line, at regular intervals of about a second. Meanwhile, the Operator issues directions using only the words 'left' or 'right'. These should be interpreted from the point of

view of the *card* Snake rather than the human one, who may well be facing a different way (as indeed he is in our picture below).

The Snake must respond by turning the next card 90 degrees in the direction specified, then continue to lay cards in a straight line until the next direction is given. The aim is to keep going for as long as possible (ideally until all cards have been placed) without the Snake running into itself, into the boundary or into an obstacle.

How to play: mongoose attack version

In this variant, the players compete fiercely (but good-naturedly) against each other, rather than working together. One player is the snake, the other a snake-eating Mongoose.

The Snake starts by placing ten cards in a line on the playing surface, keeping hold of the rest of the pack. On 'Go!', the Snake lays down the remaining cards in a line one by one as fast as possible, while the Mongoose races to gather them up from behind, starting at the tip of the 'tail'. If the Snake reaches the end of the pack with more than five cards still laid down he lives to slither another day. Any fewer, and it's no longer a case of 'Snakes Alive'.

TIP: *The number of cards the Snake starts with may be changed depending on the relative speeds of the players. And if further adjustment is needed, either player can be slowed down by being allowed the use of only one hand.*

GOING FURTHER

If there are four players on hand, you can recreate the classic digital lightcycle game **Tron**. Players must try to use their snake to force their opponent into a position where they can't move without crashing into themselves, into obstacles, or into the other snake.

Snapper in the middle

5+

Players

Indoor/Outdoor

Party game

Digital camera

One player is in the middle of a ring of other players, and has to photograph them all – while blindfolded.

| SET UP 5 mins | PLAY TIME 10+ mins | YOU NEED a camera or camera phone |

This fast, entertaining camera game has all party-goers taking part – and everyone gets a chance to be the 'snapper in the middle'. All you need is a digital camera or, if you don't have one handy, a mobile phone with a built-in camera. However, mobile phones tend to have a longer lag between pressing the button and taking the photo.

Setting up

Each player takes it in turn to be the snapper. They wear a blindfold (see page 223) and hold a digital camera, switched on and ready to shoot.

The other players stand equally spaced in a loose ring around the snapper, about two metres away. The game is best played with at least five players, so that there's a minimum of four around the snapper.

How to play

The players in the circle now declare themselves in turn in alphabetical name order. To do this, they grab an ear with each hand and pull a silly face, while calling out 'Here I am, snapper in the middle!'. They then count down from ten to zero as fast as they can, and put their arms down.

As soon as the snapper hears them, he or she has to turn to face the direction of the player who's called out and try to take a photo of them with their hands on their ears. Because the snapper is blindfolded, it's not as simple as it sounds.

When the first player in the circle has said their phrase, the next player (in alphabetical order) takes their turn to grab their ears and shout out 'Here I am, snapper in the middle. Ten nine eight seven six five four three two one zero!'

How to score the game

At the end of each round, when all the encircling players have called out and been photographed, the snapper takes the blindfold off, and the photos are inspected.

Score 10 points for each photographed 'hand on ear'. So with a total of 5 encircling players the maximum score is 100 points.

Once the score has been totted up, the camera and blindfold are handed to a new player, who takes their turn in the middle of the ring and to tries to beat the previous high score.

The end result

As well as being an exciting party game, you'll end up with a bunch of lively, interesting photos of kids and their friends pulling silly faces.

Print them out as going-home presents from a party, or post them on Facebook for everyone to share.

TIP: *It's a good idea to use a type of blindfold that can easily be removed and put back on, such as a sleepmask, since kids are somewhat prone to pulling their blindfold off to look at each photo.*

Space Invaders: table edition

Defend your side of the table from a relentless onslaught of 2p invaders.

| SET UP 5 mins | PLAY TIME 10+ mins | YOU NEED a collection of 1p and 2p coins |

One of the all-time great video games, *Space Invaders* was simple in concept but never failed to get the adrenalin flowing.

In our version, we strip away the technology, using nothing more than a handful of coins and a table.

Setting up

One player is the Defender, using 32 1p coins as ammunition, while the other plays the Invaders, using 16 2p coins. The Invaders are laid out in four rows of four coins, with rows offset so the coins in one row are between the coins in the adjacent ones. The distance between coins in the same row should match that between the player's index and little fingers. The gap between different rows should be about the same.

The Defender faces the Invaders at the opposite side of the table, their force mustered in a single pile, awaiting mobilisation.

How to play

The invading player uses the index and little finger of each hand to move one row of four coins a few centimetres down the table.

The Defender attacks the Invaders with a minimum of two and a maximum of four shots. They do this by flicking 1p coins from their edge of the table. Any 2p pieces that are struck by a 1p coin are removed from play. If a 2p 'spaceship' is hit and crashes into another, that is also destroyed and removed.

When the Defender declares their turn over (after 2, 3 or 4 shots), the invading player advances another row of 2p coins. Only one row may be moved at a time, and all the coins in that row must be moved.

GOING FURTHER

There are plenty of possible variations. For instance, there could be more than one spaceship attack per round. Or the invading player could be allowed to choose how to range his forces at the start, rather than using a 4 x 4 formation.

Many of the games in this book are newly invented, which is why we've included a notes section in the back so that you can come up with your own refinements and even (dare we say it) improvements.

The Mother Ship

The invaders have a Mother Ship (a 50p piece) which can be used once in each round. This starts from the back of the table and each go moves forward twice as far as usual, accompanied for dramatic effect by a suitably menacing noise emitted by the invading player. Other play ceases when the Mother Ship is attacking. The defending player is allowed only one shot per move while the Mother Ship is advancing, and if she reaches the far side of the table, the Invaders win the game.

Victory

If the defender hits all the attacking 2p coins before any reach his or her side of the table, a new round begins, with the defender having four fewer 1p coins at their disposal. A further four coins are removed for each successive round.

If the Defender runs out of ammunition before the Invaders are defeated, the Invader wins and they swap roles for the next game.

All ages

2+

Players

Outdoor

Active

Stopwatch/timer

Speed camera race

Race around the garden without getting caught by the bright yellow speed cameras.

SET UP 10+ mins | **PLAY TIME 20+ mins** | **YOU NEED** old cereal boxes • stopwatch

The telltale flash, alerting you that you've just passed a speed camera at 33mph in a 30mph zone and will shortly be getting a very expensive photograph in the post, is one of the less pleasing aspects of modern motoring. Here's a game that puts the ubiquitous yellow sentries to better use.

Setting up

You'll need some empty cardboard boxes – cereal boxes are fine. Paint them yellow, unless your family are fans of Crunchy Nut Cornflakes or Weetabix, in which case they'll be yellow already. If you're feeling artistic, you can also paint a speed camera symbol on the side. If not, you can download one we prepared earlier and stick it on:

fg-21.com/speedcamera.jpg

Mark out a course in the garden. This can either be straight, motorway-style, or more of a winding, country-road shape. Set out the boxes at intervals, either buried in a hedge or simply placed on the ground. These are the cameras the racers must out for.

How to play

Stopwatch in hand (every mobile phone has one), the appointed controller sets the contestants off one at a time. They must run as fast as they can to the end of the course, except when they're passing a speed camera, at which point they must slow down and walk heel-to-toe for exactly ten paces. Once they're clear of the speed camera's lens they can start to run again.

GOING FURTHER

If you're playing this game with a large number of children, there's no reason why two or even three players shouldn't all set off at once — as long as someone is checking they don't speed past the cameras.

The controller monitors the race, making sure each contestant sticks to the course and performs a minimum of ten heel-to-toe paces in front of the cameras. If players are caught 'speeding', they get three, six or nine penalty points on their licence, depending on the severity of their offence. Each point translates into one extra second added to their time. Anyone racking up 12 penalty points loses their licence and has to go off and do the washing up.

Once all competitors have completed the course, the controller announces the times, not forgetting to add on the penalty seconds. The winner is the fastest motorist still in possession of their licence.

Age 11+

Speed texting

2+

Players

Who's the fastest texter in your family? Find out with the authorized speed texting challenge.

Indoor

| SET UP 2 mins | PLAY TIME 37.28 seconds, if you're quick | YOU NEED a mobile phone |

Mobile phone

To most children, few things are sadder than a parent trying to be cool by using text message abbreviations (omg!). However, both generations can compete on a level playing field with competitive texting. Here, proper English reigns and abbreviations are forbidden.

The world record for texting a complicated 25-word phrase with no mistakes, and without using predictive text, was 67 seconds in 2005. Then it came down to 48 seconds until, in 2009, 21-year-old Norwegian Sonja Kristiansen set a new record of just 37.28 seconds. Quite extraordinary, when you consider that the message always used in these record attempts is:

'The razor-toothed piranhas of the genera Serrasalmus and Pygocentrus are the most ferocious freshwater fish in the world. In reality, they seldom attack a human.'

If you want to try your hand at it, we've prepared a large print version for you to download and print out:

fg-21.com/speed.jpg

Family texting race

Even to text-addicted teenagers, it is a major challenge to complete the phrase perfectly, let alone get anywhere near the record. If it all gets too much, you can always choose simpler phrases. As long as everybody texts the same words, nobody has an unfair advantage. It's up to you whether to allow a practice round.

Freestyle texting

There is another record for texting an *unseen* 160-character text. Again, no mistakes are permitted, and all lower- and upper-case letters must be reproduced correctly. The record at the time of writing is held by American Chris Young, with a time of 62.3 seconds.

Blindfold texting

Another enjoyable challenge is to text blindfold. The record for texting a prepared 160-character message while blindfolded is 45 seconds, held by New Zealander Elliot Nicholls since 2007.

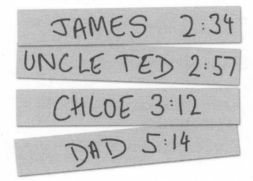

Top Piranha wall chart

Instead of using the complicated piranha phrase as a head-to-head challenge, treat it as a time trial.

Family members and visitors can ask to be tested at any time. Their error-free time should be written on a piece of card and stuck with Blu-tak to a wall chart, much like *Top Gear* does for its small-car time trials. At all times, the current champion and time will be visible. Our best time is just under four minutes, over six times the record.

GOING FURTHER

If you want to practise, it might help to know that 'piranhas' is 7, 4(press twice), 7(press three times), 2, 6(press twice), 4(press twice), 2, 7(press four times).

From the archives...

What's the time, Mr Wolf?

A terrifyingly tense game for little players.

A wolf, usually an adult, stands with their back to the players, who chant, 'What's the time, Mr Wolf?' The Wolf turns and shouts out the time in the form of something o'clock. Whatever hour is chosen is the number of paces the players must take towards the Wolf.

As players near the wolf, they also near the moment when the Wolf will respond, 'Dinner time!' and chase them, screaming, back to the safety of the starting line.

Bucket bonanza

Make children work for their party prizes.

Put supplies that would go into party bags into different buckets. To win a prize, the children must throw a tennis ball into the bucket. Decrease the distance each time they fail until they succeed.

Who is it?

An identity-guessing party game.

One player is 'It', blindfolded, in the centre. The others form a circle around them. 'It' counts to ten, while other players swap places.

'It' points and the player indicated must make noises, trying not to give away who they are. If their identity is guessed, they become 'It'. Otherwise 'It' has to point elsewhere.

See page 223 for a helpful guide to making blindfolds.

Go fish

A card game popular with young players.

If two or three are playing, each is dealt seven cards; if more, then five each. The remaining cards go into the centre.

Players aim to get four cards of the same value. In turn, they ask other players if they have any of a particular value, of which they must have at least one. All cards of that value must be handed over. If they have none, they say, 'Go fish', and the disappointed player picks a card from the central pile.

Four cards of the same value comprise a 'book' and are put down face up. The game ends when the cards run out, the player with the most books winning.

Mirror drawing

How well can you draw if you are only able to look in a mirror?

A player is given a subject to draw. But they are handicapped by not being allowed to look at the paper directly. Instead they must view it in a mirror, either on a wall or propped up on a table.

The drawing player should remain standing, and hold the paper against their body as pictured.

This can be made still more difficult by introducing an egg-timer and by requiring players to label the object using mirror writing. Each player can suggest the object for the next player to draw.

Whose picture is the most recognisable? Whose is the funniest?

Thumb wars

Two players complete in thumb-to-thumb gladiatorial warfare.

With their four fingers curled back, players interlock hands, usually right hand to right hand.

Together, moving their thumbs from side to side, they chant, '1–2–3–4, I declare a thumb war'. The first person to press down their opponent's thumb with their own thumb, and keep it held down, is the victor.

British bulldog

A rambunctious outdoor game (no bulldogs required).

Ideally played by upwards of six players, this game requires a large playing area with two safe zones at opposite sides.

One player is the 'bulldog', patrolling the ground between the safe areas. Players must run from one side to the other and avoid being tagged by the bulldog. Anybody touched becomes a bulldog and holds hands with the existing bulldog to catch other players, the chain extending as more players are caught. The winner is the last player to remain free.

Players may become exuberant during British Bulldog. As a result, it is a game best played on a soft surface such as grass or sand.

Sprouts – the dots game

Two players draw lines between pairs of dots, each trying to ensnare the other.

SET UP 2 mins | PLAY TIME 5+ mins | YOU NEED computer with internet or pen & paper

Indoor

Remote friends

Brain power

The game of 'Sprouts' was invented by two mathematicians at Cambridge University in 1967. It can be played on a sheet of paper, but if there's no one at home to play it with you, it's easy and just as fun to play online, using the collaborative drawing website **Dabbleboard**. See page 214 for full details of how to get started with Dabbleboard.

How to play

The first player draws two dots anywhere on the page. If you're using Dabbleboard, then dots are tricky to draw; we suggest drawing tiny circles instead (click the Freehand button to make this easier).

Join the two circles with a straight line or a curve, and draw another dot or circle anywhere along this new line. This is what you might get (we've numbered the dots in order of drawing, but you don't do this):

The second player now has to join any pair of dots with a single line, again adding a new dot to the middle of the new line. Let's say they loop all the way around from dot 3 to dot 1, and along this line they draw dot 4:

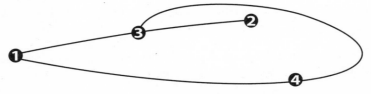

112

Each player adds a new line and a new dot along it. But this is where **Rule 1** comes in: *No dot can have more than three lines coming out of it.* The first player can't use dot 3, as this already has three lines. So they might join 1 and 4, placing a new dot at 5:

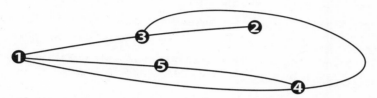

Now, the second player continues. Dots 1, 3 and 4 are now out of action, as they touch three lines already. So they join dots 2 and 5:

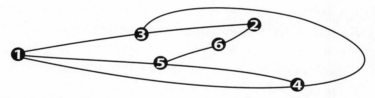

Time for **Rule 2**: *No line can cross any other line.* The first player can join dots 6 and 2 with a new line, even though they're joined already:

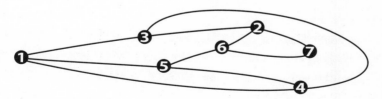

The second player is now stuck. Although dot 7 only has two lines coming from it, there isn't another free dot to connect it to – and so player 1 wins the game.

Quick to learn, this game can provide many hours of enjoyment as players learn the strategies involved.

HOW IT WORKS

Since the game was invented by two mathematicians, you'd expect them to figure out the game-play with a formula.

If a game starts with **n** dots and lasts for **m** moves, and if we call the used-up dots **p**, then:

n+m = 3n-m + 2(3n-m)+p

Which simplifies to:

m = 2n + p/4.

We hope this makes things clearer.

Spy CCTV Challenge

2+

Players

Indoor/Outdoor

![Active]

Active

Beat the cardboard CCTV camera to retrieve top-secret documents without being spotted.

| SET UP 10 mins | PLAY TIME 15+ mins | YOU NEED an old cereal box |

We've all seen spy films where the secret agent has to retrieve a top-secret document from a heavily guarded room, dodging the security cameras and timing his actions to avoid being caught. Now you can relive that excitement at home, using nothing more high-tech than an old cereal box.

Setting up

The key to this game is to ensure that whichever player is chosen to be the CCTV camera can't see outside a narrow, blinkered field of view. They could just hold their hands either side of their face to limit their field of vision, but there's a much better way.

Take an old cereal box and cut off both ends to give a hollow rectangular tube. The player sticks his or her face into one end, so that they can only see out of the other. The box may well stay in place by itself, but if not you can tie it with string or just hold it with your hand.

How to play

The camera player stands in the middle of the garden, while the other players hide indoors or behind a tree. Near the camera player are a range of objects that have to be 'stolen' by the other players, without being seen by the camera.

The camera looks straight ahead, and counts up to three out loud. He or she then swivels 90 degrees, counts to three again, then swivels another 90 degrees, and so on. Whoever is playing the camera cannot turn their head or cheat in any other way, but must keep facing in the specified direction for the full count.

The other players have to sneak in when the camera is facing away from them, grab the goodies on offer, and make their escape back to hidden safety – all without being spotted.

If the game proves too easy, then change the period of time for which the camera faces in each direction – it could be as little as one second. Or, if it's too hard, lengthen the time to five seconds. It can be fun to play the game so that only one object has to be retrieved in each turn, and the camera speeds up by counting one second less after each object has been taken away.

It adds further to the enjoyment if suitable props are used as the objects to be stolen away: for instance, documents with 'top secret' written on them, toy necklaces and other jewellery, as well as government-classified secret weapons. You'd be amazed how binoculars, cameras and even old car parts can take on a whole new significance when they become objects of international intrigue.

GOING FURTHER

For a harder challenge, add a second CCTV security guard. Both guards should start at right angles to each other, and rotate in the same direction at the same time.

2+

Players

Indoor

Computer

Street View scavenger

Use Google Street View to set fiendish scavenger hunts for your family and friends (and anyone else online).

| SET UP 15 mins | PLAY TIME 20+ mins | YOU NEED computer with internet |

You can have an outdoor scavenger hunt whatever the weather, thanks to Google Street View (see page 218). Each player takes deliberately cryptic or obscure screen grabs of objects within a set playing area and sends the others off in search of them.

Setting up the game

A good place to set your first scavenger hunt is in your own neighbour-hood. Look around within Street View and, when you find something interesting, manoeuvre around and zoom in until you think it's devil-ishly tricky to work out what and where it is, then take a screen grab (see page 226). Flowers, building materials, signs, doors – anything is grist to your mill so long as it's distinctive.

Crop your screen grab to show just a detail of the whole image. Of course, it's sensible to avoid things of which there could be more than one in the same road, such as parking restriction signs. When you've assembled all your clues, print them out or email them to all the other players taking part in the game.

The sort of close-up they must locate

How to play

Players may either work alone or in groups to locate all the objects you've photographed. They do so by navigating around the set playing area (this can be just one street, or a larger space), peering virtually around them until they discover everything you've snapped – and taking a screen grab of each entire object to prove that they've found it.

Although the game can be played there and then, another way is to email photos to players, perhaps also giving them clues as to where they should be looking. Aim to make it tricky but not impossible.

Where else can you play?

With so many countries already snapped by Google, there is a near infinite number of places to choose from. Within the UK, as well as almost every road in the land, Street View also covers attractions such as Legoland, Thorpe Park and Alton Towers. Try playing with places where you're about to go on holiday, or where you've just been.

Textoku

The brand new words and numbers game where you get to set the Sudoku-style puzzles.

SET UP 5 mins | **PLAY TIME 15+ mins** | **YOU NEED** a mobile phone or our printout

Begin by drawing a 4 × 4 grid on a sheet of paper. Or, if you prefer, you can download a whole sheet of grids here:

fg-21.com/textoku

Start filling in the grid by writing a single four-letter word across the top – in our example, we chose 'cake'. Then write a four letter word down the left side that begins with the same letter, and then place two more words into the grid. Each one should be a four letter, well known word.

Scribble out any spaces that can't be filled to make new words, as shown here.

Change the letters to numbers

This is where the game becomes more high-tech. Look at the keypad on your mobile phone, and write out the grid again, this time changing each letter to the equivalent number on the keypad, so 'C' becomes '2', and so on. If you don't have a mobile phone, we've printed a keypad for you to download here:

fg-21.com/mobile.jpg

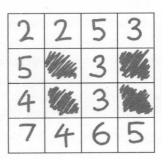

How to play

Give the completed number grid to the other players, who then have to figure out all the words in the grid. If only two people are playing, then while you're compiling your grid, the other player should be compiling theirs as well, so you can both solve them at the same time.

The easiest way to solve the puzzle, as in Sudoku, is to write all the possibilities next to each number, and see which make real words. So with the numbers given, the top row might read 'BAKE', or 'BALE', or 'ABLE', for example.

The challenge is to pick one of these words and try to fill in the rest of the grid, taking the letters represented by the numbers already in place. It's tricky, but not as hard as you might think: ten minutes' puzzling is usually enough to solve each grid.

Accept alternatives

Sometimes it's possible to complete the grid with different letters to those originally thought of. As long as real words are used, this is perfectly permissible.

In this example, if we start off with 'BAKE' as the first word across the top, we're still able to finish the grid off per-

fectly, as 'CLIP' now becomes 'BLIP' – both valid words.

GOING FURTHER

Fancy a challenge? Try working with a 5 x 5 grid, or even larger if you think you're up to the mark.

From the archives...

Coin shuffle

Players grip coins between their knees and drop them into a receptacle.

Divide the group into teams, each with a pile of coins. One at a time, players must grip as many coins as they dare between their knees and shuffle across to a cup or mug of water to drop them in, without using their hands. Players only have one chance: any coins that don't make it to the mug don't count.

The water is necessary to prevent the coin from bouncing back out.

Players old enough to recall the movie *The Dam Busters* may wish to sing the theme as they prepare to release their ammunition.

The winning team is the one with the most coins in the mug at the end.

Conkers

That most traditional of all British children's games.

Collect up horse chestnuts as they fall towards the end of summer and the onset of autumn. Make a hole in each, top to bottom, and thread a length of string through it, tying a substantial knot at one end.

One player holds their conker steady while the other flicks their conker at it, hoping to damage it. They continue as long as they keep hitting their opponent's conker, steadying the string beforehand if need be. If a player moves their target conker, a penalty-free hit goes to the other player.

As soon as the conker is missed, it becomes the other player's turn.

Local rules apply when a conker is grazed, rather than struck firmly, often with the first player to shout 'tipsies' getting control.

All serious conker players give their conkers numbers, which are the sum of its victories and the victories of all it has beaten. A 'twoser' beating a 'sixer' becomes a 'nineser' (an extra one is added for the victory).

Squeak, piggy, squeak

A classic porcine party game for younger players.

All the players sit in a ring on chairs, except one who stands in the middle. He or she is blindfolded (see page 223).

After being spun around three times, the blindfolded player finds the nearest person and sits on their lap. The owner of the lap must then make squeaking noises, while the blindfolded player has to guess who it is.

Catch and drop

A game of catch utilising forfeits if the ball is dropped.

Players form a circle and throw the ball randomly to others. Any player dropping the ball is handicapped in defined stages. If they subsequently catch it, however, they undo the handicaps one at a time.

For the first drop, one hand must go behind their back; for the second, they must also stand on one leg. A third failure sees them dropping to one knee; a fourth, to both knees. With a fifth drop, they must close one eyem while a sixth drop means they are out of the game. Each successful catch reverses the most recent handicap.

Sardines

A cram-in-the-cupboard game for parties.

In this version of hide and seek, one player runs to hide while the others count to 100. The game is best played indoors, so the number of hiding places is limited: cupboards under the stairs, behind a sofa, or in the shower are all popular.

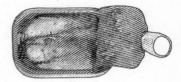

Once the first seeker finds the hidden person, they do not reveal their position, but join them in the hiding place. Play continues until all the players are squeezed into the same tiny space.

Two racing games

A brace of thrilling games for children's parties.

In *Three Legged Race*, pairs of players are tied together at one ankle, and have to race co-operatively to beat the other linked players.

In *Wheelbarrow Race*, players are again in pairs. One holds the other's legs, as they run on their hands to the finish.

Toast Busters

A test of marksmanship in which the only thing that gets shot is a piece of stale bread.

| SET UP 2 mins | PLAY TIME 5+ mins | YOU NEED a toaster • rubber bands • stale bread |

If you burn the toast or discover the bread is simply past its munch-by date and sprouting mould, don't throw it away. Instead, call out the Toast Busters. Their mission, should they accept it, is to lie in wait with rubber bands, ready to hit a piece of toast as it pops up.

This is hunting for food at its most humane: no animals are harmed and the carbon footprint is tiny (unless you burn the toast).

Setting up

Cut a narrow rectangular piece of bread and place it vertically in your pop-up toaster. Arm your Toast Busters with rubber bands that can be distinguished from each other by colour or size. Place the shooters within easy firing distance of the toaster. Let the younger Toast Busters stand nearer than their older siblings, but it's reaction speed rather than strength that will be tested here.

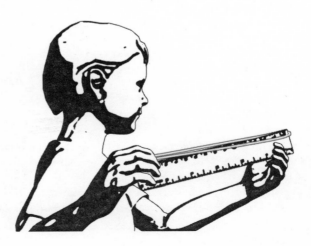

How to play

Start the toaster going. Bear in mind that as toast usually takes two minutes, so you may want to reduce the toasting time to its lowest setting. The Toast Busters wait, rubber bands stretched in anticipation, ready to let fly as the toast makes a break for it.

There are two recommended ways to fire a rubber band. The most impressive is to extend your first finger forwards and your thumb vertically, keeping your other fingers curled into your palm. With your other hand, put the rubber band over the end of your first finger, take it around your thumb and stretch it down and hook it over your little finger. To fire, just flex your little finger.

But for greater accuracy, nothing beats the old schoolboy trick of stretching a rubber band over the length of a ruler and firing it off the end. Experience has shown that the average family has fewer rulers than children, however, so you may need to improvise.

NOTE: *If a rubber band finds its way into the toaster, remove it immediately. Nobody loves the smell of burning rubber in the morning.*

GOING FURTHER

If you find your Toast Busters can't bear the wait, you can always press the Eject or Cancel button (most toasters have one) to make the toast pop up on demand. You will, of course, be in the firing line when you do this. Don't say we didn't warn you.

Top drawer: Monsters' tea party

Take turns to place ogres and elves around the table – but don't put them next to each other.

| SET UP 5 mins | PLAY TIME 10+ mins | YOU NEED our printed board • a handful of coins |

This two-player game can be played either with our printed game board, or using the online drawing program Dabbleboard (see page 214).

If playing on paper, download this board to play it on:

fg-21.com/monsters.jpg

If playing with Dabbleboard, load up this version:

fg-21.com/d-monsters.jpg

Each player has a stack of coins. One has 1p coins (the elves) and the other has 2p coins (the ogres), and they take it in turns to seat them at the table.

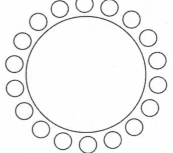

The first player places a 1p 'elf' coin anywhere on the seating plan around the circular table. The second player then places a 2p 'ogre' coin on the table, anywhere as long as it isn't next to an elf.

Play continues with the players placing coins in turn. The only rule is this: *You can't place an elf next to an ogre, or an ogre next to an elf.* The game is won when one player is unable to seat either an elf or an ogre at the table.

The Dabbleboard version

If playing with Dabbleboard, there's no need to draw coins. Each player has a different ink colour, and simply draws a stroke or a blob in the circle they want to fill.

Top drawer: Domino chess

A game of strategy where you place dominoes on a chessboard to trap your opponent.

SET UP 10 mins | **PLAY TIME 5+ mins** | **YOU NEED** our board or a chess board • dominoes

This two-player game can be played with our game board, a chessboard, or online, using Dabbleboard (see page 214).

2
Players

If playing on paper, download this board to play it on:

fg-21.com/domino.jpg

If playing with Dabbleboard, load up this version:

fg-21.com/d-domino.jpg

Indoor

Each player takes it in turn to place a domino on the chess board, spanning two squares, anywhere they like. The first player can only place dominoes horizontally (East-West), the second can only place them vertically (North-South).

The winner is the player who leaves his opponent unable to place any more pieces.

You don't have to use dominoes: cut pieces of card large enough to cover two chess squares as an alternative.

Remote friends

The Dabbleboard version

If playing with Dabbleboard, you don't need the dominoes – or a chessboard. Turn Freehand mode off (see page 214), and make sure each player is using a different colour. Then each player can just draw a rectangle (or, easier to draw, a triangle) that occupies the two squares on which they choose to place their pieces.

125

Age 8+

Top drawer: more remote games

Even more drawing games you can play with absent friends over the internet.

2+
Players

Indoor

| SET UP 5 mins | PLAY TIME 15+ mins | YOU NEED two computers with internet access |

The dot game

In the paper version you start by drawing a rectangular grid of dots. On Dabbleboard (see page 214) dots are a touch fiddly. You *can* draw a line and shrink it, then turn on the grid by using the wheel symbol at the top right, copy your dots and place each one exactly in position on the page.

Remote friends

Far easier, however, to use our prepared dot grid:

fg-21.com/dots.jpg

In Dabbleboard, click the 'insert image' symbol and type in the address above to place it on the page. You can then play over the top of that.

Player take it in turns to join two dots. The aim is to complete 'boxes' by filling in the last line, while trying to prevent your rival from doing the same. Completed boxes are marked with the player's initial, and that player gets another turn. The winner is the player who has the most initials at the end. With freehand turned off, Dabbleboard will keep the lines neat, but drawing your initials in the boxes is difficult – instead, type them in, using the type tool above the whiteboard.

Doodle bugs

One player chooses what to draw, be it a spider or a skyscraper. With freehand mode enabled, the other player begins by drawing the first element. They then take it in turns to draw the picture, with what emerges usually being very different than either envisaged at the out-set. There are no losers, except perhaps the art world.

Grumpy words

This is a great game of fitting words into a grid. First place our grid onto your Dabbleboard, using the 'insert image' symbol:

fg-21.com/grid

The first player then types a word any-where in the grid, either vertically or hori-zontally. Using at least one letter already on the board, the next player follows, and so on. Players are allowed to use vowels as often as they like, but each consonant may only be used once. The loser is the first to get stuck.

TIP: *Use the largest text size and one text box per word. For vertical words, insert two returns between letters; for horizontal words, two or three spaces.*

Picture Perfect

In this visual version of Charades, the drawing player thinks of the title of a book, play, TV show or movie, then draws one long dash for each word in the title. Short words like 'a', 'an' and 'the' may be typed out to make it easier for the guesser.

The drawing player then draws either the entire phrase or single words at a time. No letters or numbers can be used. The guessing player races to guess the missing words, typing each guess onto the whiteboard. If a word is guessed correctly, the drawing player writes it in place. If it is wrong, he or she strikes a line through it. It's a great way to hone your drawing and/or telepathy skills.

GOING FURTHER

There's no reason why four or more players shouldn't use Dabbleboard to play a virtual version of the commercial game Pictionary, as long as all players have the cards to hand.

Simply divide into teams of two, and take it in turns to draw pictures to be guessed by your teammate, using a stopwatch to set a one-minute time limit for each round.

Rather than trying to recreate a Dabble version of the Pictionary board, make the winner the first team to get to 10 or 20 correct guesses. Players should go through all the categories on one card before moving on to the next.

Age 8+

2+

Players

Indoor

![Television icon]

Television

TV bingo

Make even the most boring TV programme fun by guessing which words will crop up most frequently.

SET UP 20 mins | **PLAY TIME 15+ mins** | **YOU NEED** a TV, radio or computer with internet

If you've ever seen a Word or Tag Cloud on a blog page, you'll get the idea behind this game. They show how often particular topics get mentioned. TV Bingo does the same, only at a more detailed level.

Depending on the sort of programme, some words will crop up more frequently than others. Predicting them is a great way to involve the entire family. Whether it's the news, the latest reality show or even Gran's favourite soap, playing this game helps to reduce those tedious squabbles over which channel to watch.

Setting up

Before the programme starts, family members take turns to choose words. Go around in turn until everyone has chosen three. Clearly, *News at Ten* will feature quite a different set of words than either *Coronation Street* or *Skins*. If the game is to be played with the news, allow younger family members to take a look at that day's newspaper or a news website to get an idea of what's going on.

Words like 'the' or 'and' are forbidden but you may decide to allow verbal tics such as 'well', which is how most journalists start their replies when interviewed about the latest story they're covering.

As an example, in the first five minutes of an *Eastenders* episode, Peggy Mitchell said 'oi' five times, 'darling' three times, and 'ain't' twice. The Queen's Christmas Message is a particular favourite for playing TV Bingo, especially as it's only 10 minutes long and seems to be considered essential viewing by many families. Words like 'visit', 'family', 'children' and 'peace' crop up often – though surprisingly Her Majesty has never uttered the word 'corgi' in any of her festive messages.

GOING FURTHER

For something where you can plan ahead, such as the Queen's Christmas Message, you could make up traditional grid-shaped bingo cards, using words in place of numbers. Players listen out for the words on their grid and shade them in as they hear them. The first person to have a complete line (horizontal, vertical or diagonal) shaded in shouts 'Bingo!' and wins the game.

How to play

When the programme starts, each player has to listen out for their chosen words. They score a point each time one is mentioned. Players keep score on a piece of paper.

Bear in mind that you don't have to watch a show live. Thanks to services such as the BBC's iPlayer or Channel 4's 4oD, you can play the game whenever you choose.

Variations

You don't have to be in front of the TV to play this game. It's also a great way to turn unwitting family members into live entertainment by saying things you know will prompt a set reaction. For example, call a slice of cake 'moist' and you can guarantee Aunt Lydia will boom 'Ugh! Horrible word, "moist", horrible!' That's two points if you had 'horrible' on your list, three if you had 'word' as well.

We would not encourage it, of course, but this game can also be played (quietly) at school during lessons.

What is it?

All ages

2+

Players

Indoor/Outdoor

Creative

Digital camera

Players race to identify everyday objects from a series of extreme close-up views.

| SET UP 2+ mins | PLAY TIME 5+ mins | YOU NEED a digital camera |

Even the most familiar object can be virtually unidentifiable when seen up close. Our game that capitalises on this idea and can be played by groups of any size, appealing to younger and older players alike.

Setting up

Appoint a Quizmaster (or Quizmasters – they can take it in turns) who takes three photographs of each object they want to include in their round, making sure they're things everyone will recognise when they see them in full.

The first should be shot close up and from an unfamiliar angle, so that it's very difficult to identify what the object is. The second should be a little less obscure, but still far from clear. The third and final photo should reveal the item in its entirety.

Make sure you're happy with all three shots before moving on to another item, as every picture you keep on the camera will be used in the game.

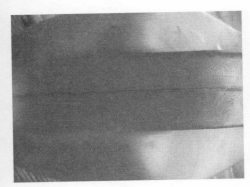

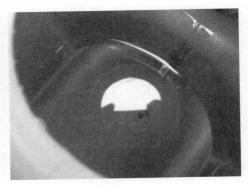

When the Quizmaster has snapped perhaps ten objects, they should link their camera to the TV (see page 212) or download the photos to their computer.

How to play

The contestants sit facing the TV or computer screen, fingers on buzzers (anything that makes a sudden noise can be used as a 'buzzer' – see the tip on page 137). The Quizmaster then displays the pictures in the order they took them, which means that each object will be shown first in its most disguised form, then a little more clearly, before finally being fully revealed. Meanwhile the players compete to guess its identity. Anybody making a wrong guess should be penalised a point to induce an element of caution.

Video version

The game can also be played with a video camera, slowly zooming out until one of the players recognises what they're seeing. If you're watching on a TV, it's easiest to burn the films onto a DVD first, with different 'chapters' for each object. Or you can use a computer, provided the screen is large enough for all contestants get a clear view.

GOING FURTHER

A high-speed version of this game is a great way to entertain a young child during a spare five minutes – and all you need is a digital camera or a camera-equipped mobile phone.

Go off into a different room and take your three pics or video, then return to show them, using the screen on the camera or phone.

Taken some particularly cunning close-ups? Can others guess them?

fg-21.com/forum

What the Google?!

Guess the most popular ways to finish a phrase – have you got your finger on the pulse?

| SET UP 2 mins | PLAY TIME 15+ mins | YOU NEED computer with internet |

Type a word, the start of a phrase or the beginning of a question into Google, without pressing Return, and beneath the search box will pop up a list of the most common searches starting with that word.

NOTE: *This game doesn't worth with Google Instant. To turn it off, either a) sign out of Google, or b) click the arrow next to 'Instant is on' to disable it.*

How to play

The Quizmaster visits *google.co.uk*, and types in a word or a short phrase. Let's say the words typed in are 'Do elephants'. Here's the (rather odd) list that Google popped up when we tried:

Do elephants pray
Do elephants have knees
Do elephants climb trees
Do elephants have teeth
Do elephants live in the jungle
Do elephants cry
Do elephants live in the rain forest
Do elephants forget
Do elephants sleep
Do elephants eat peanuts

Each player in turn guesses a phrase that might appear in the list, scoring points depending where in the list the phrase comes. The top hit scores 10 points and the bottom one point.

Suppose the first player says 'cry'. *Do elephants cry* – the sixth phrase on the list – scores five points. Players may pass if they get stuck. If any player says a phrase that *doesn't* appear on the list, they lose a point (negative scores are normal early in the game).

The Quizmaster may choose to give points for near misses. If a phrase appears more than once (*Star Wars* and *Star Wars Soundtrack*, for instance), it's the highest hit that scores.

Buying clues

At any point, a player can choose to buy a clue. A one-word clue will cost them one point, a two-word clue two points, or a three-word clue three points. So if a player buys a one-word clue for the phrase 'Do elephants', the Quizmaster might say 'joint' to help them get *have knees*; a three-word clue could lead the Quizmaster to say something like 'hinged leg joint'. If a player buys a clue but still doesn't know the answer, they can pass – and the next player is free to make use of it. At any time the Quizmaster can choose to end the round, whereupon a new word or phrase is typed in and play begins afresh, with a new player becoming Quizmaster.

What to type in

Here are a few suggestions for the type of phrases to search for:

Who invented	*Love is*	*How to make a*
How fast is a	*Pasta a la*	*Anyone for*
Never	*The stupidest*	*Mad as*
Is it rude to	*Why do spiders*	*What is the opposite of*
Complete and utter	*Beautiful*	*Do the French*

You can also search for first names: who are the top ten people called Peter, or John, or Elizabeth? The possibilities are endless.

GOING FURTHER

To make the game even harder, try typing just a single letter into Google. What are the top hits beginning with B, for instance? This version of the game is really a test of how well contestants know the big commercial players of the online world.

Found a particularly good Googling combination? Share it online!

fg-21.com/forum

133

Wikipedia game

Think laterally and use your general knowledge to jump from one word to another with the fewest leaps.

SET UP 5 mins | **PLAY TIME 15+ mins** | **YOU NEED** computer with internet access

Wikipedia is often praised for being the best, most up-to-date, and most enjoyable encyclopedia on the web. In the Wikipedia Game, we make use of one of its most addictive features to take players on an unpredictable voyage of discovery and connection.

Setting up

To play the racing version described below, both players will need a computer. Otherwise the game can be played on a single machine, as a co-operative venture. It's even fun to play alone if no one else is around.

How to play

One player chooses a starting point – for example, *toothbrush* – and the other player chooses an end point – say, *bison*. The two need have nothing to do with each other; in fact it's better if they don't. The best way to play is if each player thinks of their topic independently, without telling the other.

Both players now visit *wikipedia.org* and type the starting point into the search box, taking them straight to that page. Beginning at the same time, they must now race to get from here to the end point as quickly as possible, navigating from one entry to another using only the hyperlinks on the page.

The trick is to find entries that you think will lead in the right direction. So, in our example, scrolling down the *toothbrush* page shows us:

> The rather advanced design had a bone handle with holes bored into it for the Siberian Boar hair bristles. <u>Boar</u> wasn't an ideal material; it retained <u>bacteria</u>, it didn't dry well, and the bristles would often fall out of the brush.

The underlined words shown here are hyperlinks. Either *boar* or *bacteria* are heading in the right direction: they're both closer to *bison* than a toothbrush is. *Boar* might lead to a list of animals, but let's see what happens when we click *bacteria* and jump to that Wikipedia entry. As we scroll down the page, we come to:

> In industry, bacteria are important in <u>sewage treatment</u>, the production of <u>cheese</u> and <u>yoghurt</u> through <u>fermentation</u>

Now we're starting to get somewhere. Cheese comes from milk, which comes from cows, which are related to *bison*, right? So let's follow the *cheese* link:

> Cheese consists of proteins and fat from <u>milk</u>, usually the milk of <u>cows</u>, <u>buffalo</u>, <u>goats</u>, or <u>sheep</u>.

Nearly there! Following the *cows* link redirects to the Wikipedia entry on *cattle*, where we read…

> Hybrids can also occur between taurine cattle and either species of <u>bison</u> (for example, the <u>beefalo</u> breed), which some authors consider to be in the genus Bos as well.

Mission accomplished: we just have to click on the word *bison* and we're done. We've gone from *toothbrush* to *bison* in only three steps.

Not all Wikipedia journeys are quite so straightforward. If we wanted to get from *toothbrush* to, say, *The Simpsons*, we might notice that the first patent for a toothbrush was granted to someone in the *United States*, so we'd click the *United States* link to look for a link to an an entry on *US Television*, which might then lead us to *The Simpsons*.

The fun of this game is using your general knowledge to think laterally: how can you link the seemingly unlinkable in the fewest possible number of jumps?

GOING FURTHER

This game is inspired by **Six Degrees of Separation**, the idea that every person on the planet is just six connections away from any other. Playing the Wikipedia Game using only people is an entertaining and sometimes difficult alternative — but you'd be amazed how often, in cyberspace as on earth, it takes six leaps or less to get from one person to anyone else.

Zebra 93272

Use your phone keypad to play two great new guessing games that exercise the brain cells.

SET UP 5 mins | **PLAY TIME 20+ mins** | **YOU NEED** a mobile or printout for each player

Everyone likes a quiz. Here's a novel spin on a familiar quiz game that uses the alphanumeric keypad on a mobile phone.

Setting up

One player is the Quizmaster. Everyone has a mobile phone, but they don't need to be turned on: players simply need to be able to see the keypad. If there aren't enough phones to go around you can easily draw one for reference. If that's too much bother, we've made a downloadable version of it for you here:

fg-21.com/mobile.jpg

We've included the phone twice on each sheet, so after printing it out cut it down the middle to make two.

How to play: the standard version

The Quizmaster chooses a word that everyone will have heard of. Using his or her own phone or printed sheet, the Quizmaster then looks up the *letters* on the keypad, but reads out the *numbers* that go with that letter. He or she also helps the contestants by giving a general idea of the category of object they are trying to guess.

So if the word is 'zebra', then the number announced is '93272', and the category given might be 'animal'. The number can be written on a sheet of paper or blackboard so that everyone can remember what it is. The players then try to work out the correct answer, with the Quizmaster giving hints if they get stuck. The winner is the first player to guess correctly, who then becomes Quizmaster for the next round.

How to play: the genius version

Here the Quizmaster chooses a more complicated, longer word (say 'barracuda' – '227722832') and gives a category ('sea creature'). The contestants then take it in turn to ask questions about the mystery word, which the Quizmaster answers *in numbers only*, using the technique (or should that be 'textnique'?) oulined above. The questions should be answerable with one or two words only, but *not* with 'Yes' or 'No'. So in this instance 'Where does it live?' would be allowed, and could be answered 'ocean' ('62326'), but 'Is it a fish?' would not be permitted.

The first player to arrive at the correct word is the winner, and gets to set their own challenge as Quizmaster in the next round.

TIP: *We find that multi-player quizzes are more fun if the contestants use makeshift 'buzzers' instead of simply shouting out their answers. These can be as low-tech as the human larynx (a shriek, perhaps, or an oink), or if a more cutting-edge solution is preferred, try using the built-in ring tones or the 'sound record' function on mobile phones.*

GOING FURTHER

This game can also be played with a dictionary. In this version, the Quizmaster gives the original clue in the same way — with a number derived from the phone keypad.

However, instead of answering the contestants' questions, he or she then slowly reads out the word's definition from the dictionary.

The winner is the first contestant to guess the right answer. Wrong guesses result in immediate disqualification!

fun *(n.)*: 1. a source of enjoyment, amusement, diversion, etc.

2. pleasure, gaiety, or merriment.

3. jest or sport.

Animation for beginners

1+

Players

Indoor

Creative

Digital camera

Computer

Create your own short animated films using a digital camera and video editing software.

TIME 30+ mins | **DIFFICULTY ★★★** | **YOU NEED** video camera • movie editing software

Most family video cameras are used only for recording special events, holidays and the like. However, making your own animated movies together is immense fun. A great way to dip your toe in the water – and harness the younger imaginations in the family – is with stop-motion video, the method used to animate Nick Park's *Wallace & Gromit* films.

What you need

When we made our first animation a decade ago, our video camera used tape and couldn't be connected to a computer; editing therefore had to be done in the camera, which was somewhat challenging.

These days, you don't even need a video camera to make excellent stop-motion films. One frame at a time can be shot on a regular camera, with all the frames subsequently being linked together on the computer to produce the illusion of movement.

All you need is a digital camera and a video editing program, such as iMovie (which comes free with the Mac) or JPGVideo for the PC – see page 234 for details.

Preparation

Part of the enjoyment is in the planning. Try not to be too ambitious at first. Our very first attempt simply involved a tower of building blocks growing by itself and the result seemed like magic. Or, as seen below, you could animate a pair of shoes walking on their own.

How to do it

Animating shoes is so simple that we were able to email a video of it to our friends within 15 minutes. It is just a series of photos seen in quick succession – the digital equivalent of a flipbook.

Attach the camera firmly to a tripod. Avoid using the zoom: that way, if the camera does get knocked, you can easily reset it by comparing the shot in the viewfinder with the photos already taken. If you do make a mistake, deleting the photos immediately will save you time later.

Take a photo, move a shoe slightly, take another, move the shoe again and so on, until you've reached the end of your sequence. Cinema movies are made with 24 frames a second, but to create a convincing impression of movement you only really need 10 photos or so per second of film.

When you're done, turn to page 234 or page 236 to find out how to use your shots to create a movie; then to page 228 to learn how to upload it to YouTube.

GOING FURTHER

Many modern home video cameras now have a dedicated stop motion feature.

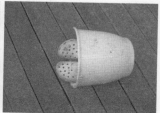

Animation: taking it further

Making your first stop-motion video will probably only whet your appetite for doing more.

The standard stop-motion video is pretty labour intensive. It took Nick Park six years to finish *A Grand Day Out*. So to start with you'll probably want to keep your animated movies short. Here are a few ideas:

- Animate a garden hose. Innocuous when on the reel, you can turn it into a scary snake by having it creep along the ground on its own. Try splicing stop-motion with a live-action sequence and have the hose sneak up on children in a paddling pool then suddenly squirt water to soak them.

- Have somebody who is partly dressed stand still as others dress them inch by inch, moving out of the way as the shutter is pressed. It will look as though the clothes are putting themselves on.

- Make a stop-motion film of somebody's drawing as they create it. Just get them to move their hand out of the frame as each photo is taken and it will look as if the artwork is drawing itself.

- Create a movie using Post-It Notes. Cover a board with them, using a single colour for the background and other colours to create simple objects which can be made to move around.

- Make your own version of *Toy Story* by bringing toys to life. Take a shot, move the subject a little, take another and so on.

Plasticine: the secret movie star

If you decide to make films with a stronger narrative, you may find it useful to buy in a supply of Plasticine. It's extremely malleable, available in many colours, and can be stiffened with invisible pipe cleaners. Using Plasticine, Nick Park has won four Oscars for his 'claymation' movies – though having wonderful characters and absorbing stories has played a big part and is every bit as important as the visuals.

Brickfilms

Another useful material for stop-motion movies is Lego. Although Lego characters are not as flexible as those made from Plasticine, they can still gesticulate and move about. And building houses, sets and vehicles from Lego requires rather less artistic skill than using Plasticine.

Our second stop-motion film after the self-building tower of bricks was a movie set on the moon using Lego and some black cotton to pull vehicles and make them land and take off.

Lego movies, uploaded to YouTube, are known as Brickfilms and often parody, or pay homage to, well-known feature films.

Non-stop Motion Video

In the past, the aim of animation has usually been to make the subjects of the films appear to move in a realistic manner, by moving whatever you're photographing only in small incremental steps.

However, a new style is becoming increasingly popular which does not require the subject to stop moving. This is much more impressionistic: photographs are simply taken at regular intervals. Rather than having 10 pictures for each second of the movie, you might have only one for each second, or use even longer intervals.

Try following somebody around, clicking the shutter repeatedly as they dress, clean their teeth, cook or even slump in front of the TV. Animate the photographs in the same way as other stop-motion video. The result will have a certain jerky charm, and it is extraordinary how well the brain fills in the gaps to interpret what is going on.

GOING FURTHER

Made what you think is a terrific movie? Compete with your friends by uploading them to YouTube (see page 228), and see whose film gets the most number of hits.

Put your best animations on YouTube — and post a link on the forum.

fg-21.com/forum

Age 8+

2+

Players

Indoor

Brain power

Calculator

Boobie shoes day

Create whole sentences using nothing but an upside-down old calculator.

TIME 10+ mins | DIFFICULTY ★★★ | YOU NEED a cheap calculator

What do Giles, Bill and Leo have in common? Why are bees, geese and hogs similar? And what links your your legs, your shoes and your soles? The answer: they're all words that can be spelled on a calculator.

The trick is to turn your calculator the other way up – you'd be amazed how many words can be spelled out using upside-down numbers.

How to play

Each player needs a calculator. Mobile phones with their more modern displays don't work: our game relies on old-fashioned calculators that are still stuck in a 'seven-segment-display' time-warp.

To play the game, the Quizmaster first makes a sentence from the words opposite (or any others they can come up with), then devises calculations that will result in the numbers that produce each word. Each player is then given a simple sum to work out. When they're done, they turn their calculators around and read out the words in turn.

For example, if you have four players, you could give them the following calculations:

Player 1:   12345 + 41371   (answer: 53716)
Player 2:   28554 × 2   (answer: 57108)
Player 3:   15.952611 ÷ 3   (answer: 5.317537)
Player 4:   40000 − 4994   (answer: 35006)

The result, when the calculations are all read out in turn, is: 'Giles boils Leslie's goose.' Now it's up to you to use your ingenuity to create your own calculations.

144

Here's a list of our favourite calculator words. Many can be turned into plurals by adding a 5 at the beginning:

GOING FURTHER

You can give one or two players a string of calculations to be performed in sequence, and get them to write down the words produced after each sum. That way it's easy to build longer sentences: 'HIS HELLISH BOSS IS LEGLESS', etc.

BE ... 38	EEL ... 733	HIS ... 514	LOIS ... 5107
BEE ... 338	EGG ... 663	HISS ... 5514	LOOSE ... 35007
BEG ... 638	EGGSHELL ... V	HISSES ... 535514	LOSE ... 3507
BEIGE ... 36138	EGO ... 0.63	HOB ... 804	LOSS ... 5507
BELIES ... 531738	ELIGIBLE ... 37816173	HOBBIES ... 5318804	OBESE ... 35380
BELL ... 7738	ELISE ... 35173	HOBO ... 0.804	OBLIGE ... 361780
BELLE ... 37738	ELOISE ... 351073	HOE ... 304	OBOE ... 3080
BELLIES ... 5317738	ELSE ... 3573	HOG ... 604	OBSESS ... 553580
BESIEGE ... 3631538	GEESE ... 35336	HOLE ... 3704	OGLE ... 3760
BESS ... 5538	GEL ... 736	HOLES ... 53704	OIL ... 710
BIB ... 818	GIG ... 616	HOSE ... 3504	OLLIE ... 31770
BIBLE ... 37818	GIGGLE ... 376616	IBIS ... 5181	OOZE ... 3200
BIG ... 618	GILES ... 53716	IGLOO ... 0.0761	SEE ... 335
BIGGISH ... 4516618	GILL ... 7716	ILL ... 771	SEIZE ... 32135
BILE ... 3718	GISELLE ... 3773516	ILLEGIBLE ... 378163771	SELL ... 7735
BILGE ... 36718	GLEE ... 3376	IS ... 51	SHE ... 345
BILL ... 7718	GLIB ... 8176	ISIS ... 5151	SHELL ... 77345
BILLIE ... 317718	GLOB ... 8076	ISLE ... 3751	SHOE ... 3045
BLESS ... 55378	GLOBE ... 38076	LEE ... 337	SHOO ... 0.045
BLISS ... 55178	GLOSS ... 55076	LEG ... 637	SIEGE ... 36315
BLOB ... 8078	GO ... 0.6	LEGIBLE ... 3781637	SIGH ... 4615
BLOG ... 6078	GOB ... 806	LEGLESS ... 5537637	SILL ... 7715
BOB ... 808	GOBBLE ... 378806	LEGO ... 0.637	SILO ... 0.715
BOBBIE ... 318808	GOES ... 5306	LEO ... 0.37	SIS ... 515
BOG ... 608	GOGGLE ... 376606	LESLIE ... 317537	SIZE ... 3215
BOGGLE ... 376608	GOO ... 0.06	LESS ... 5537	SIZZLE ... 372215
BOGIE ... 31608	GOOGLE ... 376006	LIBEL ... 73817	SLEIGH ... 461375
BOIL ... 7108	GOOSE ... 35006	LIE ... 317	SLOB ... 8075
BOO ... 0.08	HE ... 34	LILIES ... 531717	SLOG ... 6075
BOOBIES ... 5318008	HEEL ... 7334	LILLIE ... 317717	SO ... 0.5
BOOBLESS ... 55378008	HELL ... 7734	LIZ ... 217	SOB ... 805
BOOBS ... 58008	HELLISH ... 4517734	LIZZIE ... 312217	SOIL ... 7105
BOOGIE ... 316008	HELLO ... 0.7734	LOB ... 807	SOLE ... 3705
BOOZE ... 32008	HI ... 14	LOBBIES ... 5318807	SOLO ... 0.705
BOSS ... 5508	HIGH ... 4614	LOG ... 607	ZOE ... 302
EBB ... 883	HILL ... 7714	LOGO ... 0.607	ZOO ... 0.02

Who would have thought that words like eggshell, illegible, Google and boogie could be made out of upside-down numbers – and it's even more amazing when they appear by the magic of sums!

2+
Players

Indoor

Brain power

Calculator

Calculated to impress

Amaze family and friends by performing complex calculations in your head faster than a calculator.

TIME 10+ mins | **DIFFICULTY ★★★** | **YOU NEED** a calculator for your victim

We take calculators so much for granted that we often forget it's sometimes easier – and quicker – to work out sums in our heads. Especially if we're sneaky and use sums where we already know how to get the answer quickly.

Trick 1: Waiting for the Number 73

Write the number 73 on a piece of paper and hide it. Get your victim to choose a four-digit number and enter it twice into a calculator. So if they think of 1234, they type in 12341234. Ask them to divide it by 137, and then to divide that answer by their original four-digit number.

Now get them to find that hidden bit of paper. The answer, every single time, will be 73. The most impressive reveal of all is if you slip the answer into your victim's pocket before you even mention you are going to do a trick.

So how is it done? The reason you can predict the answer is that multiplying any four digit number by 10,001 is the same as entering it twice on a calculator. And multiplying 73 and 137 together produces 10,001.

Trick 2: Multiplying primes

Get somebody to choose any 3-digit number, and tell you what it is. Bet them that, in your head, you can multiply it by 7, then 11, then 13 and come up with the answer before they can do it on a calculator.

They won't believe you, but 7×11×13 is 1,001 and any three-digit number multiplied by 1,001 will be the original number twice. 782, for instance, multiplied by 7, 11 and 13, is 782,782.

A variant is to multiply any 2-figure number by 3, then 7 then 13, and finally by 37. You're multiplying by a total of 10,101 which will result in the two-figure number written out three times (for example, 52×3×7×13×37 = 525,252).

Trick 3: Fibonacci rules

The most impressive calculator trick of all requires a little more effort on your victim's part. Get them to number 25 lines, in order, on a piece of paper. On the first two lines they should write any two whole numbers – explain that it will be simpler for them if they don't make the numbers too large. Two digits is fine.

On the third line, they should write the sum of those two numbers, on the next, the sum of the previous two numbers and so on, all the way up to line 25.

Pointing out that you have no idea what two numbers they chose at the start, ask them to divide the 25th number by the 24th. Throw in some mystical 'I'm getting something coming through now' mumbo-jumbo as you reveal, digit by digit – to their utter bafflement – that the answer is 1.618033989.

How does it work? What you surreptitiously got them to do was to construct what mathematicians call a Fibonacci sequence, which approaches the so-called Golden Mean (1.618…) the more numbers are added. This is why you need to put your victim though their paces by getting them to work out at least 25 rows: the more numbers in the sequence, the more accurate the result will be.

Be warned, though: this trick will only work if their calculations are correct. Otherwise that substance left on your face will be rotten egg.

Celeb heads

Create funny photographs by holding celebrity mugshots in front of your face – and dressing up to match.

TIME 45+ mins | **DIFFICULTY ★★★** | **YOU NEED** a digital camera • pictures of celebs

CDs have been around for almost 30 years, but many people have hung onto vinyl records, as much for the sleeve art as for anything else. Witness the online craze for 'sleeve heads' – dressing up like musicians and taking imaginative and funny photographs of real life/sleeve art combos (try a Google Image search for some amazing examples). But there's no need to stick to album covers.

Dressing like celebs

For genuine sleeve heads, you need to find some interesting albums to work with. If none are lurking at home, you can pick them up cheaply at charity shops or simply print them out from the internet, where there are many sites featuring nothing else. You can also find CD sleeves online, which can be enlarged and printed out at a more practical 'celeb head' size than the originals.

The naffest and most bizarre-looking records often have the most celeb head potential. Faces work best, but other body parts can also be used. To achieve A-list celeb head status you will need to match your outfit exactly with the model's. The background is also crucial, the challenge being to find the spot that most closely fits the original setting.

Alternatively, you can use your imagination to place the celeb in intriguing or wacky locations and situations – or wearing clothes they wouldn't be seen dead in. Perhaps Bruce Springsteen in Micky Mouse Y-Fronts or Madonna in Peppa Pig pyjamas?

Getting the photo right

A bit of adjustment is necessary to get the celeb and the live subject into the correct positions. With a piece of card or paper held in front of their face, the person being photographed obviously can't see what's going on, so will need to take guidance from the person with the camera.

It is possible to make a sleeve head on your own, using a camera with a self-timer. But it's tricky unless the pose is simple, though you could try using a webcam or camera built into your computer so you can use the on-screen image to adjust your position.

Celeb head universe

Why restrict yourself to album art? Use magazine covers or search online to find photos of your favourite celebrities. Or plunder centuries of portrait art – how about a Mona Lisa celeb head? You can always use a free picture editing program to crop pictures if the original isn't quite suitable. When printing out images, use heavy paper or card if possible, or stick them to something stiff before the shoot begins.

GOING FURTHER

Instead of holding a photograph up in front of your face, why not magic yourself into the position of a celebrity by replacing their face with yours? We teach you how on page 10.

We'd love to see the shots you come up with. Post them on the forum.

fg-21.com/forum

Age 8+

Cloud catching

1+

Players

Capture clouds and combine them with everyday objects to create surreal photographic masterpieces.

| TIME 15+ mins | DIFFICULTY ★★★ | YOU NEED a digital camera • toys and other objects |

Outdoor

Instead of merely looking at clouds and remarking on their resemblance to faces, dolphins or monsters, why not immortalise that similarity by incorporating it into photographs?

Creative

This isn't the sort of photograph you can plan easily in advance. That perfect cloud can appear at any time – then it's a question of rushing indoors to find a suitable receptacle or fluffy toy that will sit happily next to it, before charging back outside, hoping that your cloud hasn't drifted away and that you've remembered to recharge the camera since the last time you used it.

Digital camera

GOING FURTHER

There are several great sources of cloud photographs on the internet. Some of our favourite are on this flickr group:

fg-21.com/cloud

Marvel at what the experts manage to achieve — it may well give you the inspiration to produce your own masterpieces.

Of course, you *could* just wait outdoors with a toy gun until a cloud that looks like a plume of fired smoke happens to drift over your garden, but you'd need more patience than we have .

Among examples we've taken or seen that we've been especially pleased with are:

- People eating clouds
- Chimney pots producing 'smoke' that's really a cloud
- A finger shooting forth a straight contrail from a jet
- Toy animals breathing out smoke
- A deflating balloon releasing a plume of cloud
- A car-like cloud with two wheels held under it
- A bottle fizzing out a spray composed of cloud.

Managed to take a really good cloud shot? Share it with the world.

fg-21.com/forum

All ages

1+

Players

Indoor

Brain power

Digital camera

Do-it-yourself instant jigsaw

Make your own photographic jigsaws in seconds, using a home shredder.

TIME 20+ mins | **DIFFICULTY ★★★** | **YOU NEED** old photographs • a document shredder

Jigsaws are great family entertainment, but after a while staple images such as kittens in baskets can become tiresome.

Luckily, there's an easy way to make your own jigsaws using your photographs, or indeed any other picure you don't mind cutting into ribbons. There's no cost and no fiddly carving with a craft knife – and, best of all, each jigsaw takes only a second or two to make.

So how is it done?

First, choose a photograph that can be cut up. It should have some clear, recognisable elements in it, such as faces and bodies – unless your family is jigsaw-mad, in which case photographs of piles of jelly beans or fields of corn may well be your thing.

Make sure the photograph you're about to destroy isn't a priceless and unique piece of the family archive. Check with a responsible adult, even if you are a responsible adult.

Get shredding

Slide the photograph into your home shredder, which will slice it into around 24 narrow vertical strips. Pick them up carefully, and place them all face up on a clean table. Slide them around a bit to make sure they're jumbled up. All that's required now is to rearrange the strips in order, to reconstruct the original picture.

Anything else we need to know?

If you're printing the photographs out yourself, it's best if you use proper glossy photo paper in your inkjet printer. Not because it matters

a great deal about the quality of the photograph, but because the thicker and more glossy the paper is, the easier it will be to rearrange the strips without them bending or curling up.

Because these pieces won't lock together like a commercial jigsaw, a slightly different strategy is required to assemble it. Rather than starting with the corners, then adding the sides and finally the middle, with a shredded jigsaw it's best to start with a discrete central area, such as as a face, building it up in strips until it's complete.

Then add the rest gradually, working outwards on either side of the completed area. The reason this works best is that it's hard to move a whole set of strips around without disordering them. So although one person could work on one bit of the puzzle while someone else works on another, it may prove tricky to join the two together later.

I don't have a shredder!

No problem. Any picture can be turned into a jigsaw merely by slicing it up with a pair of long, sharp scissors. You can even add variation by cutting into irregular shapes rather than strips, which makes the jigsaw easier to solve, and works well with smaller children.

GOING FURTHER

If you really like a challenge, try shredding two pictures and then mixing up the strips. This doubles the difficulty for serious puzzle-solvers.

Age 8+

2+
Players

Outdoor

Creative

Video camera

Do-it-yourself superhero movie

Arm yourself with a set of astounding superpowers, using just a little ingenuity.

> **TIME 60+ mins** | **DIFFICULTY ★★★** | **YOU NEED** a video camera and various props

One of Steven Spielberg's earliest home movies involved a load of cherries in a pressure cooker, which was then made to explode on film. His parents were clearly more tolerant of such devastation in their kitchen than many would be. Fortunately, there are some home-made special effects that involve rather less mess and danger.

Flying

One of our early films was called *Superbaby* and came about simply because Simon's youngest was the proud owner of a Superman costume. Suitably attired, she was put in a baby bouncer and held by someone outside the camera frame. 'Superbaby' thus magically flew – although with a bouncier motion than is normally associated with superheroes.

These days, with digital recording and editing, it is rather easier to fake a character flying.

You'll need to make a dummy to do the 'flying'. It'll be moving fast, so there's no need for it to be hyper-realistic – just stuff a pair of a trousers and a shirt with scrunched-up newspaper, using safety pins or gaffer tape to keep it together. The head can be made with a balloon, pinned to the clothes by the nozzle.

Lie on the ground with the camera. Have someone throw the fake superhero across the frame and pan quickly to follow it. Do it several times, filming from different angles. The images may well be blurred, but that's all to the good.

Now dress the superhero in the same clothes as the dummy. Shoot them leaping up at the start of their flight and landing at the end of it, which can just be them jumping onto the ground from a chair.

Left: a dummy thrown through the air can make a great flying sequence – especially if in the following scene, the superhero is seen wearing the same outfit. It may not look terribly convincing as a still image, but when seen in motion it does the job well.

The rest is done by editing. Start with the taking off, then cut to various shots of the body flying through the air, and end with the landing. Add whooshing sound effects or even the noise of a rocket. It won't be up to Hollywood standards, but it'll be good enough for a home audience to enjoy. The same dummy can also be used for fights (it will lose), falling out of windows and all kinds of other terrible accidents.

Death-ray eyes

On page 192, we explain how to make somebody vanish on film. You can use that for a great special effect here. Have the superhero simply blink or stare at someone and cause them to vanish, either suddenly or through a fade. It looks still more impressive if the victim shakes uncontrollably before they vanish. Add the sound of lightning or a death rattle. Or, if comedy's your thing, have the superhero make people disappear by farting at them.

Superhero powers

On page 166, we show how reversing video can make objects appear to jump into a person's hand. Have the superhero stretch out their hand and make their weapon magically jump into it. The trick is simply to get them to hold out their arm and drop the weapon, then reverse the footage with video editing software.

If you've just become a superhero, don't be shy – post your exploits online.

fg-21.com/forum

Indoor

Creative

Computer

Does my album look big in this?

Create your own unique album covers using random names and pictures.

TIME 20+ mins | **DIFFICULTY ★★★** | **YOU NEED** page layout application • internet access

While there are many great classic album covers, some look as if the artwork was put together at random. So perhaps it isn't surprising that many people on social networking sites have been bringing chance elements together to create realistic-looking covers.

Setting up

To find out the name of 'your' band, go to the main Wikipedia page. On the left hand side, click 'random article'. Whatever comes up is the name of your band. In our case, it was 'Wattia' (a genus of tachinid flies). You can also go straight to a random article by following this link:

fg-21.com/random1

Now that you have a band, you need a name for their debut album. For this, go to www.quotationspage.com and, as with Wikipedia, click on 'Random Quotes' on the left, or follow this link:

fg-21.com/random2

Find the last quotation on the page and select the title from the last few words. Our quotation was from Henry Adams: 'There is no such thing as an underestimate of average intelligence.' So our album title becomes 'Average Intelligence'.

Now you need some album art. Go to the image hosting website Flickr and their page of the most interesting pictures of the past week:

fg-21.com/random3

The third photograph on the page will be your album's cover image.

Making the cover

Now that you've got the three necessary ingredients, mix them together. You don't need anything as complicated as Photoshop. Even a relatively simple word processing program will have the ability to paste in an image and allow you to lay text on top – or try the online photo editor Pixlr (see page 230 for guidance).

So, for this illustration only, expert Steve moved over to let design klutz Simon have a go. Once he realised that, in the program he was using, 'text wrap' had to be turned off to allow text boxes to be placed over an image, it was pretty simple to put something together.

After a little experimentation with different fonts, sizes and colours, he came up with something we could easily imagine was in our record collection somewhere.

GOING FURTHER

When putting family photos and videos onto CDs or DVDs, why not get the children to design the cover art? Instead of random artwork use an image from one of the photos or take a screen grab from the video.

Age 8+

Experimental travel

2+

Players

Outdoor

Digital camera

Make sure you get off the beaten track by injecting an element of surrealist surprise into holidays and trips.

TIME half day or more | **DIFFICULTY** ★ ★ ★ | **YOU NEED** a sense of fun • a map

In 1969, French writer Georges Perec wrote a novel in which the letter 'e' never appeared, followed soon after by another in which 'e' was the only permitted vowel. In the same spirit, Joel Henry set up a Laboratory of Experimental Tourism (Latourex), producing sets of rules to help tourists have experiences out of the ordinary. Others have added to them and *Lonely Planet* has even produced an experimental travel guide.

Whether as a tourist, or closer to home, introducing rules like these can introduce variety and an element of surprise to all manner of trips.

Alphatourism

Instead of visiting the standard sights in a new city, find the first and last place or street name listed in a guide or map. Draw a straight line between them on a map. That is the route to follow.

Do this with a London A-Z map and you will be taken from Abberley Mews in Clapham to Zoffany Street in Islington, an eight-mile walk that will, by chance, take in some well-visited parts of central London.

This game can be adapted by blindfolding a family member (see page 223) and getting them to stab their finger on a map to decide where you'll go.

Monopolytourism

If you're visiting a City with a locally-adapted version of Monopoly (it is licensed in 103 countries), use the board and dice to decide where to go next. How many other tourists are likely to visit the local electric company or the city jail?

FACT BOX

Joel Henry takes his concept seriously. He visited Luxembourg for 24 hours in the company of his wife — blindfolded. He experienced the smells and sounds but could see nothing, and had the 'sights' described to him.

Mascot travel

Take a toy with you, be it a stuffed dinosaur or Barbie, and try to experience the holiday through its eyes. Take photos as if it were the main holidaymaker.

Countertourism

Visit tourist landmarks but, when you take your photographs, turn your back on them. Your photo won't show the usual views, but you may well end up with something more interesting.

Alternating travel

Whether away or taking a trip from home, start by turning right, then left, then right, and so on, until you can go no further. You may get lost, especially in a foreign city – so just turn around and turn alternately left and right to retrace your steps with ease.

Dogging the dog

Find a dog. Follow it.

Face changing photo trickery

Use an online photo editor to replace the heads in your family photographs.

TIME 30 mins | DIFFICULTY ★★★ | YOU NEED internet computer • family photos

1+
Players

Indoor

Computer

Creative

Messing around with family photos is easier and cheaper than you might think, thanks to the free online photo editor Pixlr.com (see page 230 for details). Here, we show you how to swap the heads of a girl and her dog in just five easy steps.

1. Select

Begin by opening your image in Pixlr, and use the **Lasso tool** to trace around the dog's head. You don't need to select the

whole head in one go: hold the **Shift** key to add to your selection while tracing with the Lasso. This makes it easy to select the head in chunks.

2. Copy and Paste

Use **Ctrl-C** to copy the dog's head, and **Ctrl-V** to paste it. The copy will appear in the middle of the photo, as a new **Layer**: you can see this in the **Layers palette**. We can now manipulate this layer on its own, without affecting the rest of the photograph.

3. Free Transform

Choose **Free Transform** from the **Edit** menu. You can now drag a corner handle to scale the layer (hold **Shift** to keep the proportions the same). You can also drag the layer around, and if you move the cursor just outside one of the corners it changes to an icon that allows you to rotate the layer.

4. Erase

Once the head is in place, switch to the **Eraser tool**. You can use this tool to remove unwanted parts of the head. If you click the fuzzy brush icon in the toolbar at the top, a palette opens so you can select a different sized Eraser: choose a soft brush for smooth edges.

5. Repeat

Hide the dog head layer by clicking the eye next to it in the **Layers palette**. Now you can see the whole image again, so select the girl's head and repeat the process to place it on the dog's body. Finally, click the eye again to reveal the dog's head once more.

All ages

2+

Players

Indoor/Outdoor

Creative

Digital camera

Fun family photos

Brighten up your family album with these tricks to make everyone look like they're having a good time.

TIME 10+ mins | DIFFICULTY ★★★ | YOU NEED a digital camera • a picture frame

Ready, steady, go

Almost every digital camera has a timer, so the picture-taker can fix it to a tripod, press the button, and then rush to stand with the rest of the group. The whole group looks neatly composed except for the photographer, who is usually flustered and breathless. And yet they're often the only one who doesn't look bored, so why not get everyone to do the same thing?

Gather the whole group behind the camera and then start the ten-second countdown. Everyone then has to dash into fame and pose themselves as rapidly as they can. The result is a lively, interesting shot, often with a great deal of laughter.

Get jumping

To bring a family photo to life, try jumping into the air. The photographer gets everyone to jump up on the count of three. You can't do this with a timer, unless your mental timekeeping is immaculate, but it does make for an exciting, energetic shot.

The rule of three

Cameras with a timer often also have a mode to take three pictures on the trot, rather than just one. This gives you triple the chance of getting an appealing shot.

It's also a great way to spice up family portraits. Set up the timer to take those three shots in rapid succession, but – and this is the crucial part – don't tell anyone what you're doing. The first photo might be

The original photo, left, shows everyone posing. But if everyone has to rush into frame, you get a much livelier and more interesting photograph.

as stiff and staged as ever, but then people will relax, and that's when you'll get the best results.

You'll be framed

Hold an old picture frame, without a picture, in front of your subjects when you photograph them – or they can hold the frame themselves. Most kids will instantly strike a pose when looking through a frame; it's an instant and easy way to simulate a work of art.

You can pick up old frames for a pittance from car boot sales and charity shops. The more ornate, the better.

Frames can also be an excellent way of tricking your subjects into thinking that you aren't filming them, helping you to capture them in those elusive natural poses. The knack is to hold up the frame conspicuously in the direction of one person, but cunningly point the camera viewfinder at someone else – your true subject. You'll be surprised how easily people are fooled by this simple deception (all in the name of art, of course).

Ghostly Encounters

Age 8+

1+

Players

Indoor

Creative

Computer

Fake a spooky ghost photo by placing two images with the same background on top of each other.

TIME 45 mins | **DIFFICULTY ★★★** | **YOU NEED** computer with internet • a camera

1. Take your photos

Put your camera on a tripod, and take two pictures of the same scene. One will have your 'ghost' looking spooky, the other will show someone else reacting to it (or it could just be an empty room). The tripod is important, because you have to take both shots with exactly the same background.

2. Open the photos in Pixlr

Go to the photo manupulation website Pixlr (*www.pixlr.com* – see page 230), and choose Open image. Load the first photo from your computer. Then choose **File > Open** to open the second photograph as well.

3. Copy the photo

On the second (ghost) image, choose **Edit > Select All**, then **Edit > Copy**. You can now close this photo. It will ask if you want to save changes: just say no, as there aren't any.

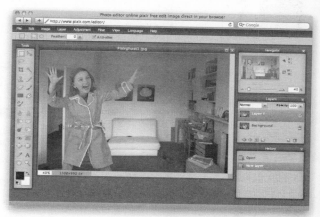

4. Paste the image

Now the first photo is the only one open. Choose **Edit > Paste**. The ghost photo will appear to replace it.

In the **Layers panel**, drag the **Opacity** slider to make it transparent. An opacity of between 50% and 60% works well.

5. Select and delete

Reducing the opacity of the ghost makes the underlying layer transparent as well. Use the **Lasso tool** to make a selection around the girl on the original photo, and delete this from the new layer: now, we can see the first girl at full opacity.

Age 11+

2+

Players

Indoor/Outdoor

Creative

Video camera

Computer

Going backwards

Shoot a scene and then reverse the footage to make ordinary actions look hilarious – or just downright odd.

| TIME 20+ mins | DIFFICULTY ★★★ | YOU NEED a video camera • movie editing software |

Film that's shown backwards can be hugely entertaining, particularly when you've shot the video specifically to be seen in reverse motion.

Although your video camera almost certainly won't let you show movies backwards, it isn't difficult to achieve the effect with a computer – check out our guide to reversing video for both PCs and Macs, on page 232.

The basic idea

It's strange but true: if you shoot film specially to be watched backwards, the results can be very impressive. All it takes is a little thought as to what's going to work well in reverse – and for whoever's being filmed to 'act backwards' wherever possible.

It's a great opportunity for family experimentation, to see what works and what doesn't. If a particular method or action isn't as rib-tickling or jaw-droppingly awesome as you expect, you'll know next time.

Tricks to try out

- Have somebody jump off a low wall and, in reverse, it will look as if they've leapt up. Try filming it with them facing the wall and bending their legs as they land. This will make the 'jump' look more realistic.

- Eating is particularly gross seen backwards – it looks as if the subject is ejecting food from their mouth. This works brilliantly with spaghetti.

- Pluck the petals from a flower one by one and, in reverse, it looks as though you're assembling the flower by hand.

- If you have some old bit of china you're about to throw out, smash it first by dropping it onto a stone paving slab: in reverse, it will appear to reconstruct itself and jump back into your hand.

- All kinds of falling objects look impressive as – shown backwards – they jump into the air. Film someone releasing a broom with their palm downwards. When the video is reversed, the broom leaps into their hand. This is great for superhero movies (see page 154).

- Crumple some paper and throw it onto a fire; seen backwards it will appear as if the paper is created in the fire, jumps out into the hand and then uncrumples itself.

- Hold two tennis balls in each hand, and throw them one at a time out of shot, then wave your hands around as if you're waiting for the balls. Seen backwards, it will look like a dramatic catching trick.

- One of our favourite tricks needs somebody willing to get wet. Get somebody else to throw a bucket of water over them. Watched backwards, the victim starts out drenched, then the water flies off them and back into the bucket, leaving them miraculously dry.

GOING FURTHER

It can also be fun to get people to do everything backwards for a time, and then reverse the footage. There's a peculiar other-worldly quality to video shot this way: it looks weird, but it's hard for the viewer to figure out exactly why.

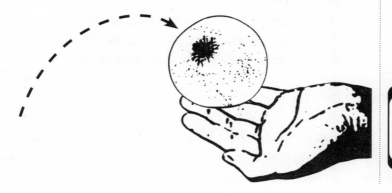

We love going backwards. And we want to see you doing it too!

fg-21.com/forum

167

The greatest card trick in the world

2+

Players

Indoor

Trick

Computer

Tease your audience for all they're worth with this glorious card trick with a sting in the tail.

TIME 15+ mins | DIFFICULTY ★★★ | YOU NEED a pack of cards • an internet connection

This is our favourite of all card tricks, because it makes the victim think you've failed completely, only for you to turn the tables when they least expect it.

Preparation

This trick requires the fall guy to pick out the five of hearts, so you must learn how to 'force' a card, as well as how to perform a convincing false shuffle.

Prepare a pack with the five of hearts on top, then divide the pack in half. With your thumbs bending the ends up, bring the corners together. Riffle your thumbs up the cards, and they will mingle together as they fall. To keep the top card in place, ensure it is the last to fall.

How to force the card

While you shuffle – ensuring that the five of hearts stays on top – boast shamelessly about the wonderful magic trick you're about to perform.

When you're done shuffling, adopt an air of superiority and ask your victim to pick a number from two to 12 and announce it to the group. If they choose 'six', methodically demonstrate what you want them to do, as though they're rather dull-witted. Slowly count out six cards from the top of the pack, placing them face down on the table, and show everyone the sixth card. Now put the *pile* back on top of the *cards* and hand it to your prey, asking them to do the same.

Providing your patter has been natural, no one will have clocked that what you've done during your demonstration is put the previous top card – the five of hearts – in the sixth position. So now when your

victim counts out their six cards, the card they reach, the sixth, will be the forced card.

Get them to show the card to everyone except you, and stress how very important it is that they remember it. Ask them to return it to the deck and shuffle the cards as many times as they like.

Look through the cards and finally, with an air of triumph, show them the *wrong* card, saying 'Is this your card?' They will gloat. Let them. Pretend to be distraught, as though you can't understand what went wrong. Don't let them tell you what their card really was.

The coup de grace

Later, when everyone has forgotten about the trick, find a cunning way to get your victim to access this website:

http://fg-21.com/footballfrenzy/index.html

It appears to be a page about football. But when they try to play the video, a message appears reading: 'Is this your card?' To their utter astonishment, the five of hearts slides in from the side of the screen.

Home movies the Hollywood way

Make proper narrative films with stories and characters – Tinseltown here we come!

| TIME 1+ hr | DIFFICULTY ★★★ | YOU NEED a video camera |

Once you've mastered making home videos and stop-motion movies, you might want to go further and really harness the family's creativity. So why not make a real movie with a plot and dialogue?

The key to success in telling any story is planning. Just pointing a camera and shooting while 'actors' make it up on the hoof may be fun at the time, but the result is likely to end up being a tedious mess.

Don't bite off more than you can chew. Aim for something no longer than 15 minutes and follow the normal rules of story, having a beginning, a longer middle, and an ending.

What sort of film is it?

As with a major movie production, as much work should go into planning the film as making it. What sort of film is it to be? In deciding, consider what costumes and props you can press into service.

- Science fiction. The sort of films that boys always seem to want to make. However, given your likely low budget for special effects you will need to be inventive (see page 154 for ideas).

- A western. If you have hobby horses and some toy sheep or cows, this can be fertile territory. If there are boys in the house, you probably won't be short of weaponry.

- An action movie. This has the advantage that dialogue is relatively unimportant, but it is fiendishly difficult to make action movies look convincing. However, the fun of making it may be more important than the end result.

- A silent movie. Has the advantage that dialogue is completely absent, though you can add captions on 'cards' later while editing. There's also plenty of suitable music available online.

- A period film. Whether you opt for knights, maidens and maybe dragons or perhaps cavemen and (plastic) dinosaurs, delving into the past could prove fruitful.

GOING FURTHER

Why not also put together a 'making of' documentary in the style of DVD extras, incorporating cod interviews with the 'stars' and perhaps even a 'blooper reel'.

Narrative

Scripts should be kept simple. They will work best if those constructing the story are able to express what the film is about in the following way: 'It's the story of X, who does Y.' This model is used by the world's most successful scriptwriters ('It's the story of a boy who discovers he's really a wizard') and if keep it in mind, you will be able to ensure your film stays focused.

And remember at all times: beginning, middle and end!

Dialogue

Keep dialogue short and sweet, and encourage your actors to learn their lines, though as a back up there's nothing wrong with having them written on 'idiot boards' held out of shot.

Filming

Just as they do with real movies, get each scene right before moving on. If there are people at a loose end who want to be involved, make a clapperboard and have them say 'Our movie, scene 3, take 5' before each shot.

For a selection of further tips that will help you to make the most of your home movies, see **The 6-Step Film Course** on page 196.

Age 5+

Honey, I blew up the kids

Create a spectacular wall covering by printing out your favourite photographs at huge sizes.

1+

Players

Indoor

Creative

Digital camera

Computer

TIME 30+ mins | DIFFICULTY ★★★ | YOU NEED computer with internet • a printer

Children like taking photographs, and most also enjoy decorating their bedroom walls – but normal-sized photos are too small to make much of an impact. It's also expensive to buy poster-sized prints online or on the high street. Luckily we've found a great – and cheap – way to create super-sized versions of favourite images. What's more, children can do it themselves using just a home printer, with the aid of a truly innovative website.

The Rasterbator

It may sound rude, but the *Rasterbator* is a website designed to help people print giant-sized prints. Rather than simply enlarging the pixels, it works by converting the picture into circular dots of varying size and spacing – this is called a 'halftone' image. The full address is *http://homokaasu.org/rasterbator*, but we've created a shortcut for you here:

fg-21.com/blowup

Using the *Rasterbator* is easy: click the Rasterbate Online button on the home page, and it will give you the choice of uploading a picture from your computer, or using an image you find on the internet. Pay heed to the warning, which helpfully states: 'Please note that the image is trans-ferred to the web server, so you probably shouldn't try to rasterbate top secret nuclear device schematics.'

First choose the image you want to enlarge (pictures with high contrast tend to work best), then use the next dialog to crop it to the desired shape. Once you've done that, press the Image Size button to set the dimensions at which you'd like to print out the image. You

GOING FURTHER

As well as simply decorating our bedroom walls, you can use the Rasterbator as the basis for a set of party games.

Remember **Pin the tail on the donkey?** Think how much more entertaining it would be if, rather than a dumb ass, players have to pin a pair of dark glasses, a false beard or a fuzzy wig on a huge blow-up of the birthday boy or girl.

Print out the photograph and fix it to the wall, or turn the making of it into another party activity, so all the guests can help to create this new 'donkey'.

need to set your paper size (A4 in the UK, Letter size in the US) then choose the number of sheets the image should be spread across. A readout at the bottom of the screen shows both the total number of sheets and the final dimensions of the whole artwork. Simply drag the corner of the image to enlarge it and preview exactly how the sheets will be divided up.

You'll then be asked to choose whether you want a colour or black-and-white image, and to set the maximum dot size. Once you've decided, press Continue. Within a few seconds, a PDF file containing all the sheets in your image will be downloaded to your computer.

Now print it out. Because home printers always have a margin around the edge of the page, it will look better if you trim away the white edges. Assemble the sheets in the right order, stick them together, and you have your giant poster.

Age 8+

2+
Players

Indoor

Brain power

Computer

Invisible e-Ink and other codes

Two simple ways of making your computer messages unreadable to prying eyes.

Computers make communication faster and easier, but they also make it harder to keep others from prying. Here are two simple ways to conceal text from casual snoopers. Both are also an enjoyable way for parents to send secret messages to their children when they're away from home.

The font code

Highlight the text of your email and change the font to one composed of symbols. Then send that instead. Obviously, the other person must have the same font installed in order to decode your message, but

174

most computers will have Symbol and Zapf Dingbats, for instance, both of which are suitable. To anyone not in the know, the message will seem complete gobbledegook.

To read the message, the recipient only has to highlight the text and change it to a normal font such as Times.

Of course, using this code is a giveaway that you're keeping something secret, unless you can convincingly pretend that you're the reincarnation of an ancient Egyptian who is fluent in hieroglyphics.

TIP: *Annoyingly, the Mail software that comes with the latest Macs makes it difficult to switch to non-Latin fonts, so use one of the many third-party word processors instead, and copy and paste it into your email.*

GOING FURTHER

You're not limited to the symbol and foreign-language fonts that come with your computer. There's a huge range of free foreign and pictorial fonts available online – our favourite source is dafont.com:

fg-21.com/font

Invisible ink

The coolest way to conceal what you're saying is to hide it in plain sight, using the modern equivalent of invisible ink.

Write a normal email but put the 'secret' informa-

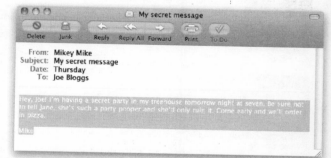

tion between the lines or at the end. Then change the colour of the hidden text from black to white. Assuming there's a white background, the text simply vanishes from view. It's as easy as that.

Use a prearranged code word or phrase in the subject line to indicate to the recipient that there is hidden text, or they might not realise. They simply use the cursor to highlight the concealed message and it will magically appear.

The technical word for sending hidden messages is steganography.

Magical photo frames

2+
Players

Indoor

Creative

Trick

Video camera

Recreate the Harry Potter moving portraits at home – and set up a great practical joke.

| TIME **60 mins** | DIFFICULTY ★★★ | YOU NEED video editing software • a movie camera |

Most Harry Potter fans wish they could have one of the magical moving portraits at home, but many people already have the capability without realising it. The secret ingredient is a digital photo frame which can display video, a much underused feature. Showing an endless video of Johnny winning the sack race might be a little OTT for all but the pushiest parents, but there are some much cleverer things you can do.

What you need

Check the specifications of the digital picture frame, and ascertain which computer video formats it accepts (e.g. mp4, avi or mov).

You'll need a way to record a short video. If you don't have a dedicated video camera, most digital cameras can do this, as can most computers with a built-in camera and many mobile phones.

You'll also need some video editing software. It can be pretty basic, as long as it will let you play video backwards. (See page 232 for instructions on how to reverse video on Macs and PCs.)

How it's done

Put the camera onto a firm base. A tripod is ideal but you can improvise if you don't have one. Shoot a short video of yourself or another family member, then upload it to your computer.

Paste the clip into your video editing software. Now paste the same clip again but keep it highlighted. Set this second clip to play backwards. This way, the clip will play forwards then backwards. Once you've set it to play in a loop, the moving clip will appear seamless.

GOING FURTHER

Digital photo frames
can also play still
photographs in order.
Use a stop-motion
sequence (see page
140) to make a simple
animated story.

Export the whole clip into one of the supported video formats and upload it to the photo frame. Set the frame to play video on repeat and, hey presto, it really looks like magic as the subject moves around within the frame.

The Digital Photo Frame Practical Joke

The video-playing capability of digital photo frames creates the opportunity for a great practical joke. Shoot a video of yourself remaining absolutely still for a time, then make just one small, sudden movement, a wink perhaps or sticking out your tongue. Loop this as above.

We've found the trick works particularly well if the frame is placed on a guest's bedside table. Imagine Gran's surprise when the cute photo of her darling granddaughter suddenly pokes out its tongue just as she's settling down to listen to *Book at Bedtime*.

Age 5+

2

Players

Indoor

Trick

Mind-reading miracles

Perplex your audience with the magical mind-reading bond that exists between parent and child.

TIME 10+ mins | DIFFICULTY ★★★ | YOU NEED sharp wits and the ability to count

These two mind-reading games can be played with an adult and a child of almost any age – or by two kids on their own. Both are easy to learn and are great fun for the mind-reading pair as they watch the mystified audience trying to puzzle out how the tricks are done.

Trick 1: How many fingers?

An adult asks a child, who can't see them, how many fingers they are holding up. Amazingly, the child is repeatedly able to come up with the correct number.

The adult holds up seven fingers and asks: 'How many fingers am I holding up?' After a moment's thought, the child responds: 'Seven.'

Now the adult holds up three fingers, and wants to know: 'How many now?' The child concentrates hard. 'Three,' they reply.

How it's done

All the child has to do is count the number of words in the question. It's the same (or should be) as the number of fingers being held up. The technique is very simple, but it still baffles audiences. Just don't let it go on so long that they cotton on – which they're less likely to do if you steer clear of low numbers.

Even very young children can manage this trick. The concentration on their face is palpable as they go painstakingly through the question, perhaps surreptitiously counting out the words on their fingers.

This is a trick we've performed with our kids for years, and it rarely fails to amaze even the most intelligent audience.

Trick 2: Name that object

In this trick, the child leaves the room and the audience selects an object; it might be a candlestick, a wine glass, or a chair – anything that can be seen in the room.

The child is called back and looks around the room as if trying to sense what has been chosen. Let's suppose it was the candlestick. The adult whose mind they're reading asks the child: 'Is it the lemonade bottle?' 'No,' says the child. 'Is it the table?' 'No.' 'Is it my shoe?' 'No.' 'Is it the candlestick?' 'Yes,' they say confidently, to a round of applause.

How it's done

The correct object is always the next one after a black object is named. There will always be plenty of black things to choose from, and the child has then only to say 'Yes' to the next item.

Unlike the finger trick, this can go on for ages before the audience works it out. They'll think they know how it's done, and perhaps suggest that it's always the fourth object. In which case let them choose which number object it should be, being sure to use a different black item. If they think you're giving a verbal signal, offer to say just one word, or even simply to point at the objects in turn. If they think you're using gestures, turn your back on the mind-reader.

For the adult asking the questions, baffling the audience is huge fun. Suggest they just use people's shoes. Then you can ask about everyone's shoes in turn, the chosen ones coming just after mentioning a black pair.

GOING FURTHER

It's easy to work out variations of the Name That Object game to test your audience still further. You might always pick the object after a round object, or after an object on legs, or after an item of food.

Just make sure you agree the rules with whoever is doing the mind-reading before they leave the room.

Photo trickery for all the family

Create amazing trick photographs while you're out and about, using nothing more sophisticated than a camera.

| TIME 10+ mins | DIFFICULTY ★★★ | YOU NEED a digital camera |

To create perfect trick photographs, first fire up your £600 copy of Photoshop, and then – no, wait! You *don't* need expensive software programs to do impressive trick photography!

Trick 1: Playing with heads

Headless body shots are easy to create if you have the right kind of terrain to work with, and are a great way to liven up country walks. In the shot on the left, one boy hid behind a tree stump, his head just poking out above it, while the other stood up facing the other way and bent his head down so it was out of sight.

In the shot on the right, the head on the ground looks as if it's lying there on its own, but in reality, the boy is lying in a slight hollow, masked by fallen leaves. As before, the upright figure has his head tucked foward.

Trick 2: Playing with scale

In the old days of film cameras, trick photography was made much harder because the viewfinder was offset from the lens: it showed roughly what you'd end up with, but not exactly. That made tricks such as this one, which relies on precisely positioning all the subjects in the frame, far more difficult to pull off.

The big advantage of today's digital cameras is that you can see the shot perfectly framed on the screen before capturing it, making it easy to line up trick shots such as this one, where the two kids in the background appear to be dancing on the adult's hand.

To set this up, the photographer needs to stand some way back – that's because if he or she is too close to the person holding their hand out, then they'll be in focus and the people in the background will be

blurred (or vice versa). The further back the photographer stands, the more of the scene will be in focus. If your camera has a zoom, then zoom in to the fullest extent and stand as far back as you can get to frame the shot.

GOING FURTHER

To make the headless shots look even more convincing, the headless person and the head should both appear to be facing the camera.

The simplest way to do this is to get them to turn their clothes round, so they're wearing their top backwards. If only the tips of the fingers are visible, no one will notice that the hands are the 'wrong' way around.

Show off your best trick photographs to other F&G readers around the world.

fg-21.com/forum

Indoor/Outdoor

Creative

Trick

Digital camera

Rotated camera trick

A simple but effective trick that needs nothing more than a little ingenuity.

TIME 15+ mins | **DIFFICULTY ★★★** | **YOU NEED** a digital camera • some props

Trick photography is always fun, and often produces surprising results – even when you think you know how it's going to turn out. Forget expensive image editing software: there's a lot you can do with just the camera on its own.

One of our favourite tricks is to take the picture as if the camera is on its side, but treat the view as if it's the right way up. This was a technique used in the early *Batman* TV series, when the Caped Crusader had to climb up the wall of a building on his bat-rope.

They simply built a wall set, and turned it sideways so that the windows were set into the floor. Then, with the camera also on its side, Batman and Robin would appear to be straining to climb the building using just the rope, when in fact they were only walking while holding the rope and leaning back slightly.

Another piece of childhood magic gone up in bat-smoke.

How it's done

You'll need to find a good location. Think laterally: what works well when turned sideways? We've used a chair lying on its back on a porch, with its legs placed against the wall.

The subject lies down, posing to appear as natural as possible. Holding a book or newspaper helps to add to the realism of the scene; if they can lift their head off the ground while you take the picture, so much the better (although you'll have to be quick, as it can be a bit of a strain). The result is a photograph that looks, at first glance, like an ordinary scene. It's only when you look closer that you notice the oddness in the background – should that field really be sideways?

GOING FURTHER

The effect can be greatly enhanced by a lot of props, if you have the time and inclination. Build sideways rooms by turning furniture on its side; if you have an old door lying around, place it flat on the ground (you'd be surprised how many people do have old doors lying around).

The chair scenario is just an example. You can use any combination of wall and floor: large stone steps outside public buildings work especially well, as they're often big enough to sit on sideways. Avoid using grass as your floor, though, as when rotated it tends not to make a convincing wall.

For extra realism, try fixing an empty drinks can to the wall with sticky tape or modelling clay. When rotated, it will look as if it's standing on the ground.

Made a great rotated camera shot? Or just want to see what others have done?

fg-21.com/forum

Say 'cheese' – in 3D

Join the 3D craze by adding an extra dimension to your photographs, with no special equipment.

| TIME 30+ mins | DIFFICULTY ★★★ | YOU NEED a digital camera • a printer |

With 3D movies all the rage, it's a shame stereoscopic still cameras have never taken off. However, with a little effort, you can create your own 3D photos at home. And you and your audience won't need special glasses.

Setting up

Your photograph should have items of interest in two planes, one being relatively near the camera. Perhaps have somebody pose nearby and place something eye-catching further away. Avoid blank walls or, if outside, indistinct backgrounds such as bushes.

Ask your subject to keep still. Take a photograph in portrait orientation (with the camera held vertically) then step to one side and take another. It is important to keep the subject in exactly the same position in the viewfinder. Try it several times to ensure you get a pair of decent shots.

Viewing the photographs

Print the best pair of photos on a single sheet. As they're in portrait orientation, set your page to landscape mode. They should be almost touching, as in the picture on the facing page. If you haven't a colour printer, it works fine in black and white.

If you don't want to print the photos, view them side by side on your computer. You may need to adjust the size at which they're displayed, so that both can be seen together.

Whether viewed on screen or printed out, hold a piece of thick paper or card between the images, with the other end touching your

Place a piece of A4 paper between these two photos, end on, one end touching the gap between them and the other touching your nose. You should be able to see the pictures as a single true 3D image.

nose. This way, each eye sees a different photo. If the images are not too large, you should get the three-dimensional effect without much effort. Like magic eye photos, you need to be patient as your eyes – which normally go cross-eyed when looking at something so close – instead need to be 'wall-eyed' or parallel.

The really lazy way of doing it

There's an even simpler way of making 3D images, and that's to go to the website Start 3D:

fg-21.com/3d

Here you can upload any photograph and view it moving from side to side, giving you a slightly different view as it shifts. They claim it only takes three minutes to get your first 3D photo on display.

Check out a few of the examples on their website – it should give you ideas for composing your own photos.

Age 8+

2+

Players

Indoor

![Brain power]

Brain power

Scytale: the wrap around code

A treasure hunt code game using a cipher invented by the ancient Greeks for their military campaigns.

| TIME 30+ mins | DIFFICULTY ★★★ | YOU NEED strips of paper • a ballpoint pen or pencil |

One of the oldest and simplest ciphers is a physical one called a scytale (it rhymes with Italy). Greek (and later Roman) military officers wound a strip of leather around a rod and wrote a message down the length of the rod. When the strip was unwrapped it displayed apprent gibberish until the recipient wound it around a rod of the same dimensions.

Coding and decoding a message

You don't need to use leather. A thin strip of ordinary paper, cut from an A4 sheet, does the job just as well. Rather than a custom-made rod, wrap the paper around a pen or pencil; the common six-sided sort are easiest to write the letters on. Wrap the paper around the pen in a spiral, and then write your message along the barrel.

If you rest the pen on a table, it should hold the paper in place while you write. If you still find it tricky, use a small piece of tape at each end to hold it firmly.

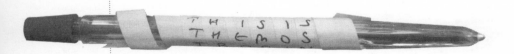

When the message is unwound, it becomes unreadable. So while the message wound around the pen above reads 'THIS IS THE MOST BORING LESSON I'VE EVER HAD', when it's taken off the pen the bemused teacher will see only 'TTTGNEHHBLIVIEOEHESMRSA-RIOISIHSSNDEAD', a message that's far less likely to get you into trouble at school.

The Scytale code game

Once the attraction of coding and decoding messages for its own sake has worn off, scytales can also be used for a treasure-hunt-type game. The trail can be followed by several people co-operatively, or by just one person on their own.

The organiser starts by giving the player or players the first scytale, on which is written a clue to the location of the next – this could be as simple as 'Look in the fridge' or 'Under the hair dryer'. Each scytale leads onto another. The final clue indicates where the prize or treasure is located.

As in a normal treasure hunt, the clues can be made more or less ingenious depending on the age and sophistication of the hunters.

Two-team variation

In this variation, players split into two teams, with each team setting a 10-clue scytale trail for the other. Take care not to be spotted hiding the clues! Teams start at the same time, and it's a race to the finish.

Age 11+

1+
Players

Indoor

Creative

Digital camera

Computer

See-through computer

An easy but impressive optical illusion that turns your computer screen transparent.

> **TIME 15+ mins** | **DIFFICULTY ★★★** | **YOU NEED** a computer • a digital camera

One of the neatest and most satisfying tricks you can do with a computer is to make the screen appear to be transparent. It's as if you can see right through it to the objects behind.

It takes a bit of effort to get this to look just right, which is a challenge that older kids often enjoy. Although you can pull it off with a desktop computer, you may have to unplug lots of cables to lug it into position. It makes more sense to experiment with a laptop, particularly as the folding screen makes the set-up process much easier.

The first photograph

Position the computer in front of an interesting background. Place some objects so they extend behind the screen and some that are entirely hidden by it.

With your camera at the ready, position yourself as close as you can to directly in line with the screen, although the photograph can be angled a fraction off centre if you wish. From that position, zoom in with the camera until the computer desktop completely fills the screen (a dedicated digital camera is better here than a phone camera). Hold that position while you, or somebody else, folds down the computer screen. With the flash turned off, now take a photograph of what's behind it. In fact, take a few with slight variations to make things easier for yourselves later.

Transfer those photographs to the computer, and then go through them, replacing the image used for the computer's desktop with each one until you find the most convincing.

The second photograph

Return to your camera and position yourself in the right place, inching sideways and up and down until the real objects around the screen are in line with the desktop image. Now take a photograph like the one below, showing not just the screen, but the keyboard and some of the background too. You'll need to play around a little with the camera position and lighting but, when you get it right, it's pretty nifty. The computer screen appears to have vanished, leaving behind only the frame, while desktop icons or folders appear to be floating in mid-air.

All hands on screen

For a really dramatic effect, photograph someone's hand in the 'view' through the screen – then get them to stand next to the computer with their hand behind it, while you take the final picture. It really does make the screen look transparent!

GOING FURTHER

The same idea can also be applied to the desktop images shown on phones. You'll need two phones: one to take the first photo, and another to take a second picture of that phone with the first photo displayed on its screen, against a wider background.

It sounds complicated, but it's not difficult once you get going – and it works particularly well with 'celeb head' style pictures of faces (see page 148).

We've shown you ours. Now show us yours!

fg-21.com/forum

189

Age 5+

2+
Players

Indoor

Creative

Computer

Sound effects

Record your own radio play, creating sound effects with a range of household objects.

> **TIME 60+ mins** | **DIFFICULTY ★★★** | **YOU NEED** a microphone • a computer

Listen to a radio play, and what really brings it to life are the sound effects. Any family can produce their own mini-play, using a selection of household items to make the sound effects. It's great fun to assemble them, trying them out as you go. The quality will be best if you have a dedicated microphone, but many gadgets can now record audio without one, such as your computer, digital camera or even mobile phone.

One person reads the script, the others make the sound-effect noises close to the microphone. Don't worry too much if you don't quite achieve perfection; getting it wrong can be part of the fun.

Here's a stirring tale of derring-do to get you started:

The story you read	**The sound effects**
It was a crisp spring morning as Sir Trotalot walked across the gravel path to his stable.	*Shake a half-empty cereal box from side to side to make the footsteps.*
In the distance, he could hear the birds in the trees.	*Make bird noises by whistling. Make the sound of flying by flapping two leather gloves together.*
When he reached the stable, he climbed onto his faithful steed, Giddyup…	*Neigh like a horse.*
…and trotted out into the stableyard.	*Coconut halves, banged together, make the ideal horse; if you don't have any, use empty yoghurt pots.*
As he trotted, it started to rain.	*Scrunch your fingers in an empty bin bag for the rain.*
Riding faster and faster, he galloped to the castle of Baron Darren.	*Drum your fingers on the lid of an empty tin for a good galloping noise.*

At the castle he slowed to a trot and stood in front of the massive drawbridge. "Baron Darren!" he called, "Your time has come!"	*Bang the coconuts or yoghurt pots together, slowing to a stop.*
The huge portcullis slid slowly up, as Sir Trotalot dismounted.	*A socket wrench, turned slowly, makes a great portcullis.*
He strode into the entrance and banged on the heavy castle door…	*Slam the lid of an empty wooden box, or jewellery box.*
… which creaked open…	*Rub two balloons together.*
… and slammed shut behind him.	*Close a microwave door for the click.*
"You won't take me alive!" said Baron Darren…	*For the boomy, echoing voice of Baron Darren, put your head in an empty box or wastepaper basket.*
… as he drew his mighty sword.	*Scrape a metal spoon over a baking tray.*
The two men fought like fury, slashing at each other with their swords…	*Scrape spoons or spatulas over the baking tray, occasionally banging them against each other and against the side.*
… and punching each other with their fists.	*Hit the table with a rolled-up newspaper.*
As they fought, Baron Darren knocked over an oil lamp…	*Drop a handful of cutlery into the baking tin.*
… and flames began to engulf the castle.	*Scrunch a foil crisp packet gently to make a great fire sound.*
"Enough!" cried Baron Darren, "You have vanquished me!" He stripped off his armour and threw himself on Sir Trotalot's mercy.	*Draw metal spoons slowly against the baking tray, and drop them onto the table.*
Sir Trotalot, knowing honour was satisfied, galloped off into the sunset…	*Coconut shells or yoghurt pots again.*
…his spurs jangling as he rode away.	*Shake a bunch of keys in rhythm with the trotting horse.*
But was it his imagination, or could he hear Baron Darren's sinister laugh behind him?	*Stick your head into an empty box and produce your most horrible laugh!*

GOING FURTHER

Get creative! Make up your own stories and invent new ways of creating sound effects.

Why not film your production as well as recording the sound? It can be entertaining watching your cast furiously banging together yoghurt pots and rattling keys.

Recorded the perfect story? Post a link to it on the forum.

fg-21.com/forum

Stop go: hey presto!

Use one of the oldest tricks in cinema history to create an instant disappearing (or appearing) act.

TIME 20+ mins | **DIFFICULTY ★★★** | **YOU NEED** a video camera

The term 'special effects' tends to conjure up images of big-budget Hollywood productions. But here's a great effect that can be produced with an ordinary home video camera – shoot a bit of film, stop shooting, alter the scene, and then start shooting again. It sounds so simple as to be hardly worth doing, but the results can be fantastic.

Ancient history

As soon as the film camera was invented, people were playing tricks with it. It's no coincidence that one of the great early film-makers, the Frenchman Georges Méliès, started his professional life as a magician.

Méliès discovered one of the most common cinema special effects by accident. He was filming a street scene when the camera jammed. Fixing it only took a moment but, when he watched the footage, he discovered that 'a bus had changed into a hearse and men changed into women'.

Over 100 years on, the 'stop trick' can still impress audiences – especially if they're watching a home movie in your sitting room rather than the latest James Cameron blockbuster. And it has the great benefit that it is an 'in camera' effect, so no extra equipment is needed.

Setting up

Make sure your video camera is fixed on a tripod, so you can be sure it won't move mid-trick. Bear in mind that the background should stay motionless between shots: this makes the appearance and disappearance of your stars all the more surprising.

How it works

Film somebody sitting in a chair. Stop the camera, and get them to move out of the scene, then start filming the empty scene again. When you play back the film, it will appear as if they have simply vanished into thin air.

Even more impressive is to have another actor walk in and drape a sheet over them. Stop the camera while the sitter gets up and leaves the frame, then drape the sheet over the chair, taking care to recreate its original position as closely as possible.

Start the camera again, and film the actor whisking the sheet away. Hey presto – no more sitting person! A small jump in the appearance of the sheet is impossible to avoid, but it shouldn't be very noticeable – especially if the second actor remains in the shot throughout as a distraction. Remember, though: they'll have to be in exactly the same pose when the camera starts again as they were when it was paused.

If you're having trouble with the sheet, try this trick with a large cardboard box, or a cupboard. And it's just as easy to make it look as if the first person has not disappeared, but turned into somebody else, or even the family pet.

Here are some more suggestions:

- Have your actors' clothes change instantly.

- Get a follically-challenged member of the family to rub some lotion into their scalp and have a long blonde wig miraculously appear.

- Have one person change into another, wearing the same clothes.

- Have your actor perform a video magic extravaganza by making a whole series of objects appear and disappear, and even change size, just by pointing at them.

GOING FURTHER

If you're prepared to put a bit more effort in, here's an impressive variation.

Set up the camera on a tripod in the garden, and have someone walk into the frame: have a chair magically appear as they sit down, then make a newspaper appear in their hands, and other pieces of furniture materialise around them as they read the paper.

It's well worth the time it takes – the end result can be spectacular.

We really love stop-go movies. Put a link to yours on the F&G forum.

fg-21.com/forum

Age 5+

Players

Indoor/Outdoor

Creative

Video camera

This is your life!

Make a movie to celebrate a significant birthday or anniversary.

| TIME 2+ hrs | DIFFICULTY ★ ★ ★ | YOU NEED a video camera • video editing software |

Next time a parent or grandparent has a major birthday or anniversary, rather than simply making a card, compile a video that celebrates the events in their life. Here are some ideas to get you started.

The interviews

Film other family members as they relate a short anecdote about the person in question. This is a great way to get grandparents to divulge secrets of what their children got up to when they were young, Set a time limit of two minutes.

What's their favourite?

There was a television game show in the 1970s called *Mr and Mrs*, in which husbands and wives were quizzed about their spouse's preferences on a range of issues.

If Dad has a birthday coming up, get Mum to one side and test her knowledge of her husband's favourite things. You might ask questions such as:

● What's Dad's favourite pudding?
● Where does Dad most like to go on holiday?
● Which three things would Dad take with him on a desert island?
● What really makes Dad cross?

Why not also ask these same questions of other members of the family? Then, when you show the film, get Dad to reveal his true preferences, and see who knows him best.

Act out the events

A highly amusing twist is to get the kids to act out key events from their parents' or grandparents' lives. It helps to enlist an adult to help work out the scenes and direct the action, but the sort of events that could be re-enacted for a wedding anniversary, for instance, might include:

- The moment they first met
- The time Dad (or Mum) proposed
- The wedding itself
- The moment they found out they were going to have a baby

Running commentary

Take a short film of the parent or grandparent performing some every-day task, such as washing up, cleaning the car, cooking, or just brushing their teeth. Then add a spoken commentary, recorded later, as if it's a major sporting event.

Of course, since you've already seen the film, you'll know exactly what's going to happen next – but hearing it 'predicted' before it actually takes place can be very funny.

Add a montage of stills

Old photographs can be put to good use in your film. One way is to arrange them on a table and pan the camera slowly along them; or you could put the camera on a tripod and place the photos down one by one in front of it.

And with video editing software, you can drag digital photos straight into the timeline – try using them during the opening title sequence, or at the end during the credits.

GOING FURTHER

Interview work colleagues and distant relatives as well as family members. They don't have to be present: hold a microphone to the earpiece of a phone as you call them up, or use an online video chat system such as Skype. Stay very quiet and try not to interrupt, as your voice will be much louder than theirs.

When you put together the film, play the recording over a still image of their face, or a picture of a telephone.

MOV

The 6-step film course

These days just about every family has the technology to shoot their own films, even if it's a mobile phone rather than a dedicated piece of hardware. But how can you turn a random group of shots of a family holiday, a football match or a birthday party into a movie people might actually want to watch?

In the old days of Super 8 cine cameras, editing was difficult and expensive. Most people simply didn't have access to the right equipment.

Today, every computer comes bundled with film-editing software, but most of us are still content to string together scene after scene with little consideration for the audience. Yet with just a little planning and know-how, that string of scenes can be edited into a slick-looking, compelling film that will silence viewers' groans and make them sit up in their seats.

Home movies 1: the perfect setup

Video cameras are wonderful for recording the important events of family life such as birthday parties and family holidays. But these films are rarely watched again because they are little more than a random selection of clips. They don't hang together like a proper film. A few simple tricks will enliven your home movies no end.

When is it?

Even if it's only by using the date stamp facility on your camera, include the date in the first shot. Otherwise, in ten years' time, you'll have no idea when it was. An alternative is to begin with a close-up of that day's newspaper, showing the date and the big headlines, and then pull back to reveal where you are. This will also help to set the historical context of the film.

Setting the scene

Plan from the outset how you would like your film to begin and end. Thanks to computer editing, you don't have to shoot the scenes in the order they'll be seen. But do try to include an establishing shot: it'll help make what follows more interesting.

- For a sporting event, film some of the training, or perhaps the kids putting on kit – or even trying to find it under the bed.

- For a family outing, video the food being prepared or the car being packed. This looks great speeded up.

- Even if you're just filming the children playing in the garden, start inside the house and walk out to 'discover' the action.

- If you're on a trip or a holiday, film a sign showing the place name and pull back, or start with a close-up of a postcard of a famous landmark, then zoom out to reveal the family standing in front of it.

- For a birthday party, begin with a card or banner. If it shows the birthday boy or girl's age, so much the better.

- Make a placard with the title of the film on it, and film a member of the family holding it on location.

Wrapping it up

The temptation after a long, tiring day is to slump. Take a bit more time and film a closing shot, perhaps everyone piling into the car to go home or the kids getting into bed, exhausted after their exertions.

Spice it up

Here are a few ideas for giving your videos more pizzazz.

- Film in the style of a news report, with somebody as reporter and other participants being interviewed. This works particularly well for sporting events.

- Make a David Attenborough-type nature documentary in the garden or the park, or even around rock pools at the beach.

- Do *Big Brother*-style interviews about how things have gone.

- Enlist someone to play a hushed investigative reporter: 'I'm here in the kitchen. In front of me, two pieces of burnt toast. Mr Rose, do you deny that you were responsible?'

Above: on a family holiday to Paris, Steve found a local newspaper with the perfect headline – 'Quel beau week-end' ('What a beautiful weekend'). The headline referred to the unseasonably warm weather.

Starting with a close-up of the headline, zooming out reveals the newspaper lying on a table with coffee and croissants.

Home movies 2: interview technique

Thanks in part to TV shows like *Big Brother*, we're all familiar with the video diary. Thousands of hapless contestants have shared their inner-most thoughts and opinions with the world. Why shouldn't we do the same? Surely at least it couldn't be any *less* interesting?!

Video blogs are one way of doing this, of course, but interviews can also be used to liven up home movies. Rather than just shooting the action, take individual family members or friends to one side and ask them to comment on the event that is taking place.

When intercut with the main footage, this approach can produce a much more personal, more engaging movie, in which we learn what the participants are thinking as well as seeing what they're doing.

These tips should help you use interviews to good effect.

Ask questions, then cut them out

When we watch any kind of interview, we expect comments from the interviewee – but what we don't want is a booming series of questions from the person behind the camera. Because they're much closer to the microphone, anything they say will be so loud as to be almost deafening.

Ask questions, by all means, but then edit some of them out when you put together the finished movie. The result will be a much smoother, much more professional feel to the film.

Cut interviews down to size

Shoot interviews for as long as you like, but don't feel you have to include every word your interviewee says. Cut their answers ruth-lessly down to just the interesting parts. Short interviews punctuate the action; long ones send your audience to sleep.

You don't have to show the interviewee while he or she is speaking – it can work well to extract the audio and run the interviews over the action or just a panoramic shot of the scene as a whole.

Home movies 3: you need a tripod

If there's one thing that makes home movies look amateurish, it's shaky camerawork. The lighter the camera, the more it will jiggle about. At the very least, tuck your elbows against your body or rest the camera on something. A small beanbag or a bunched-up jumper both do the trick, holding the camera in position and allowing the camera operator to feature in some shots.

It makes no sense having a giant tripod for a pocket-sized camera. But there are two products you might consider to ensure steady, shake-free filming.

WHERE TO BUY

Before heading straight for Amazon or eBay, try a Google search for these items. You'll be surprised at how much prices can vary, even day to day. But remember to check postage costs before clicking the 'buy' button.

Joby Gorillapod

This brilliant design has three bendy legs that can cope with irregular surfaces and wrap around objects like tree branches, railings or even bicycle handlebars. There's a wide range, some with magnetic feet. The cheapest, for small cameras, sell for under £10.

Bottle top mount

A few companies make mounts for around a tenner that screw onto a bottle. With liquid in the bottle the camera is held securely. There's

also the Bottlepod from *www.7dayshop. com*, which can be fixed to any bottle or thin vertical surface, or even a car windscreen. At the time of writing, it can be had for under a fiver, including delivery:

fg-21.com/bottlepod

Home movies 4: using the camera

Your camera may have plenty of special effects – black and white, solarizing, sepia tint, and so on – and naturally you want to play with them. But unless there's a really good reason, resist the tempation. They will simply distract your audience and you won't be able to remove them afterwards. If you need special effects, your movie editing software will let you add them at a later stage.

Zooming in and out

Constant zooming in and out is the surest way to make your audience feel queasy. By all means use the zoom to frame the shot *before* filming, but otherwise try to restrict it to zooming out to establish where you are, or zooming in to show where the action that follows in the next scene is to take place. If you do film with full zoom, make extra sure the camera is held steady or you'll end up with a seriously shaky movie.

As well as optical zoom, which adjusts the position of the lenses, most cameras also have digital zoom. This simply enlarges the pixels, giving an ugly, blocky image, which looks terrible. Avoid digital zoom at all costs!

Keep your mouth shut

Unless your commentary is part of a grand artistic plan, restrain your enthusiasm. As you're so much closer to the camera, all your audience will hear will be your booming voice. And try not to breathe too loudly.

Scenes and angles

Don't film everything from a great distance. If it's a sporting event, shoot some cheering spectators, or close-ups of players – remembering to zoom in *before* hitting record. Switching between wide shots and close-ups makes for a watchable film, and you can always edit in shots of the family cheering after a goal is scored or the finish line breasted.

Hold steady!

Torches jerk around – after all, there's no good reason to try to hold them still – but the camera shouldn't. Move it as smoothly as you can, remembering you don't have to keep your subject dead centre.

Change your position

A whole film shot from one place is tedious. Move about between scenes. You can also change the camera height, crouching down or climbing onto something to get a fresh angle.

Keep filming

Don't restrict yourself to the main event: film the preparations and aftermath. Get some close-ups – and don't forget the post-match interview. Talk to participants and take family members aside to ask their view of the proceedings. You can always edit later.

The camera is not a sniper sight

The subject does not have to be dead centre, as if viewed through a rifle sight. Try using the Rule of Thirds: imagine a noughts and crosses grid overlaid on the image. Position the subject where a vertical and horizontal line cross, and line up the horizon with one of the horizontals. Ask the subject to look straight at the camera lens: you'll find the effect is strangely harmonious.

Home movies 5: editing movies

ALL DONE?

Play the movie through several times. Are there patches you now find boring? If so, your audience will too. Trim them out. When you're happy with it, consider adding a commentary, though these are often nothing like as witty as people think they are when they record them. Captions may be more effective.

If you have the equipment and the time, print a label onto the disc, perhaps with a screen shot on it. However you choose to do it, it's essential to label it somehow for future reference, even if only using a felt marker pen.

One drawback of having high-tech digital photography and moviemaking equipment at our fingertips is the temptation to excess. But unless you edit your film down, you will quickly tire your audience. It may have been a wonderful holiday, but they still won't be keen on watching that fortnight you spent in Granada played back in what seems to be real time. Let 'brevity' always be your watchword.

What you need

There are plenty of computer movie editing packages, **iMovie** being the default program for Macs, and **Windows Movie Maker** for PCs. There are others with more features, but these should be perfectly adequate for most purposes.

Most computers can burn movies to a DVD. Blank discs cost only a few pence, so it's wise to start by copying everything on the camera to a DVD. That way, if you make an irreparable blunder, you won't have lost the only footage of some vitally important family moment.

Editing essentials

Get rid of the fat first, throwing away everything you know for sure you won't need. Treat each 'event' you film as a separate story. Using the program's subtitling feature, give it a name and date it, particularly if you didn't use the date stamp when filming.

Work on each sequence separately, dragging the clips into the timeline to edit them. You should generally start with an establishing shot, and remember to insert occasional close-ups.

The brain is amazingly good good at filling in missing details so if, for instance, it's a sandcastle-building scene, use a series of rapid cuts to show the construction process, slowing again to real time only when it's almost finished.

Home movies 6: musical glue

As well as helping to create the right mood, music can also cover up unwanted noise. The human brain tends to filter out irrelevant sounds that enter through the ears, but microphones and cameras aren't so clever: they indiscriminately pick up every gust of wind, every passing car – even the sound of the neighbours' TV. Background noise can ruin a good movie.

Add music after you've finished editing the footage, fading it at moments when you need to hear what's being said. Music can also be used to unite a series of disconnected stills, making them feel almost like a movie.

Pick the right track

If your film is for home use only, add any music you like. Choose appropriate soundtracks for the type of film you're making. Here are a few examples:

- For a holiday shot in France choose some accordion music or an old Piaf classic or two.

- If you're filming kids attempting something difficult, try the theme to *Mission Impossible* or *Dr Who*.

- If you're filming a race, try slowing it down in your movie editing software and adding the theme from *Chariots of Fire*.

- Well-chosen music can be harnessed to the cause of comedy. Try livening up family scenes with the theme music from *The Simpsons* or *The Waltons*.

If you want to expose your film to the masses and put it on YouTube, you'll need to be sure you aren't infringing copyright. Then see page 228 for how to upload your film to YouTube.

FINDING MUSIC

There are many sources of free and royalty-free music available on the internet. Check out freeplaymusic.com, as a good starting point – or, for a huge library of free music, visit freemusicarchive. com.

The internet is also a great source of low-cost sound effects. For a comprehensive range try Sounddogs:

fg-21.com/sound

And for a free archive of terrific sound effects of all kinds, we recommend the Absolute Sound Effects Archive:

fg-21.com/sound2

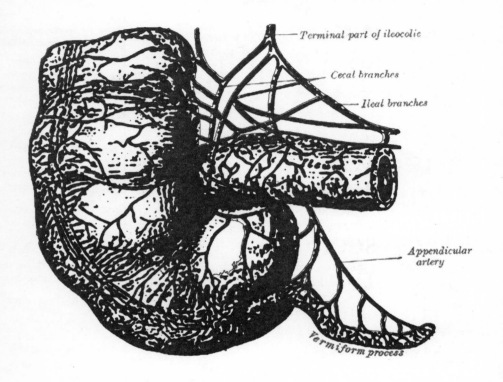

Terminal part of ileocolic

Cecal branches

Ileal branches

Appendicular artery

Vermiform process

appendix *(n.)*: 1. a vestigial lymphoid organ that extends from the lower end of the cecum and which resembles a small pouch.

2. a section or table of additional matter at the end of a book or document.

Computer dice machine: Mac

THE GAMES

Never say die,
page 60

Eat the jelly,
page 45

How to program your Mac to roll dice then declare the result.

TIME 15 mins | **DIFFICULTY ★★★** | **YOU NEED** a Mac computer

Computer programming doesn't have to be the preserve of insomniac nerds: here's a simple program everyone can write that will generate random dice numbers, then say them out loud.

The Mac dice machine

Begin by opening your **Applications** folder. Inside, you'll find another folder called **Utilities**. In there, you'll find an application called **Apple-Script Editor**: double-click it to open the application.

Type the following two lines of code into the window:

```
set rn to (random number from 1 to 6)
say rn
```

The finished window should look like this:

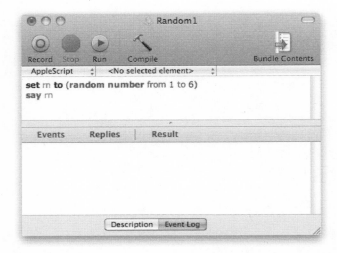

All the formatting – the colours indicating different syntax, and the bold words – will be done automatically for you. Press the **Run** button, and the program will speak a new random number each time.

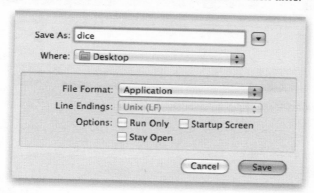

GOING FURTHER

This version of the program speaks random numbers between 1 and 6. But you could simulate dice with any number of sides, by changing the last digit in the first line to any number you like.

You can take this one stage further by saving your script as a standalone application, so you don't need to open the **AppleScript Editor** each time. Choose **Save** from the File menu, then follow these steps:

1. In the 'Save As' field type *dice* (or any other name you'd prefer for your program)

2. From the **File Format** pop-up menu, choose **Application** to make a standalone program

3. Choose where you want to save your application (e.g. your desktop) and click **Save**.

You'll now have an application called *dice* on your desktop. Each time you double-click it, it will speak a different random number between 1 and 6.

See overleaf for the Windows version.

dice

Computer dice machine: Windows

THE GAMES

Never say die,
page 60

Eat the jelly,
page 45

How to program your PC to roll dice then declare the result.

TIME 15 mins | **DIFFICULTY ★★★** | **YOU NEED** a Windows computer

On the previous spread, we showed how to program a Mac to come up with a random number between 1 and 6, and speak it to you. Here's how to do it in Windows…

The Windows dice machine

Begin by opening the **NotePad** application. Type the following text:

```
Dim message, sapi
Dim max,min
max=6
min=1
Randomize
message=(Int((max-min+1)*Rnd+min))
Set sapi=CreateObject("sapi.spvoice")
sapi.Speak message
```

You must make sure that the quote marks are straight "rabbit ears" quotes, and not curly "smart quotes", otherwise the program will not work. It should look like this:

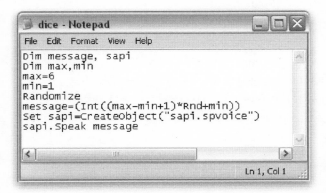

When you've typed in the text, choose **Save** from the file menu, and you'll see the standard **Save** dialog. There are now just two further steps:

1. In the **File name** field, type `dice.vbs`
2. In the **Save as type** field, click the pop-up menu and change the type from **Text Documents** to **All Files**.
3. Choose where you want to save it – say, the desktop – and press the **Save** button.

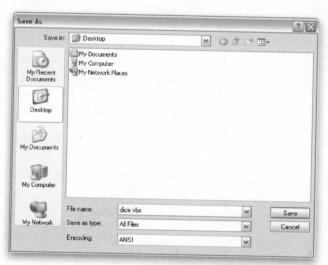

You'll now see an application on your desktop called *dice*. Double-click it, and it will speak a random number between 1 and 6 to you. Each time you double-click, it will speak a different random number.

GOING FURTHER

This version of the program speaks random numbers between 1 and 6. But you can create dice with any number of sides, by changing the 'max' value in line 3 to any number you like.

EVEN EASIER

If you really don't want to type in the code yourself, we've done it for you: go to this link, then copy and paste the whole code into Notepad:

fg-21.com/dice

Connecting your computer to a TV

THE GAMES

What is it?
page 130

Avoid having to crowd around a small computer screen by hooking your PC or Mac up to your TV.

TIME 30 mins | **DIFFICULTY ★★★** | **YOU NEED** cables to fit your equipment

You'd have thought connecting your computer to a television screen would be a straightforward business. And sometimes it is – depending what sort of sockets your television and computer have. There are three key variables: the output socket on your computer, the input socket on the television, and the cables that link them together.

The computer socket

Most PC machines have one of two sorts of socket for outputting a video signal: either an S-Video socket or a VGA socket. To make things trickier, S-Video sockets have either four or seven holes, so you need to count yours to see which variety you have.

Above: VGA socket

Left: S-Video socket

If you're using a Mac, it will use one of three different proprietary display sockets, depending on the model, and you'll need to buy a VGA adapter from Apple that matches the socket on your computer.

The television socket

Almost all televisions have one of two common input sockets. The SCART socket is the most common, and this is used mainly to hook up a video or DVD player. The other type is an RCA connection, which takes the form of three small round sockets grouped together, coloured red, yellow and white. It's usually used for connecting video cameras.

Find the cables

Assuming your computer and TV sockets fit the descriptions above, you will need one of the following four cables: VGA to SCART; VGA to RCA; S-Video to SCART; S-Video to RCA. All of these can be purchased from most high street or online computer or electronic stores.

Above: SCART plug. Below: RCA plugs

Connecting the TV to the computer

Once you have the right cables, you should be able to connect the video output from the com-puter to the video input on the television. The next stage is make the two see each other.

If you aren't using a SCART connection, which should switch auto-matically, you'll now need use the menus on your TV (accessible via the remote) to find where to change the AV input.

Check the user manual if you're having problems. Don't panic if you can't immediately lay your hands on it – you're almost certain to find it online with a quick Google search.

If you're still having difficulty, it could be because the computer screen is set to a higher resolution than the television can support. Open your **Control Panel** (Windows) or **System Preferences** (Mac) and choose a lower resolution. You may have to restart your computer with the cables plugged in.

STILL STUCK?

It is possible to connect just about any make of computer to just about any make of television. If your TV is 'HDTV Ready' you may need to use a cable with an HDMI plug, although it should still have a SCART socket as well.

If your local shop doesn't have exactly the cable you need, you may need to buy several cables and convertors and chain them together. As long as the two machines are able to connect, the signal should get through.

It's also easy to connect iPods to a TV, using cables specifically for the purpose.

Stuck? Got a problem – or a solution? Discuss it in the forum.

fg-21.com/forum

Dabbleboard: draw with distant friends

Dabbleboard (www.dabbleboard.com) is a collaborative drawing website that is free and fun to use.

TIME 15+ mins | DIFFICULTY ★★★ | YOU NEED computer with internet

We love Dabbleboard. It's the perfect way to inject some creativity and fun into a rainy day at home, allowing you and your friends to draw pictures together at the same time over the internet. Best of all,

When the 'Freehand' button is pressed, you draw as normal – otherwise, lines are smoothed out automatically

Click the 'new' icon to start a new drawing

Click the 'download' and 'print' icons to print a drawing or to download it to your computer

Click to load text or images onto the page

Images are automatically saved into your library

As well as clicking the Undo/Redo buttons, you can use the standard Undo keystroke on your computer it's absolutely free. Unusually, you don't even need to sign up to use it, although it's worth doing this (it only takes a moment) if you want to save your drawings for a later session.

We've suggested a load of games using Dabbleboard – see 'The Games' at the left of these pages. While it's an easy website to get started with, we thought we'd try to help you make the most of it with our quick guide to what all the tools and buttons do.

Choose whether to add arrowheads to your lines

Set the thickness of the lines you draw

Select a colour

Invite friends to join you by typing their email address

This circle was drawn with the 'Freehand' button off, which turned a rough sketch into a perfect circle

Every line you draw is a separate object. Select it by clicking on it, and will be highlighted with icons at the corners. Click these to delete it, rotate or flip it, scale it and move it around the page

Send text messages to your friends, or if they have a webcam you can both see and speak to them

Click anywhere to type words: press DONE or the esc key on your keyboard when you're finished

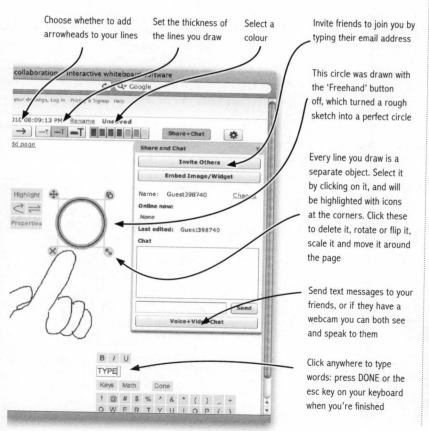

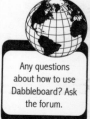

Any questions about how to use Dabbleboard? Ask the forum.

fg-21.com/forum

215

Google Earth: make your own tour

THE GAMES

Google Earth
challenge,
page 32

How to set your family and friends fiendish geographical challenges using Google Earth.

TIME 1 hour | **DIFFICULTY ★★★** | **YOU NEED** computer with internet

It's easy to make your own Google Earth Challenge. First, download Google Earth:

fg-21.com/earth

Install and open the application, then search for your first location – we've chosen the London Eye, as it's easily recognisable from the air. Zoom in to give a clear close-up view, choose **Placemark** from the **Add** menu, and type a name for it.

You don't want players to see the names of the locations you've chosen, so make a new sidebar folder to keep them all in – choose **Add > Folder**. Give it any name you like.

Add more places

Search for all the landmarks you want in your Challenge, zooming in so they're clearly identifiable, then adding a Placemark for each one. Put all your Place-marks into the Tour folder you made earlier.

Start the tour

Once all the Place-marks are in your folder, choose **Add > Tour**. Press the red **Record** button in the **Tour panel** that

appears in the bottom left corner of the main viewing window, then double-click the first Placemark to go to it.

Your tour will now be recording. Use the **Microphone** button if you'd like to add a recorded soundtrack.

Double-click the next Placemark in your Tour folder to fly to that location, then click the next Placemark, and so on until your Tour is complete. When you're done, click **Record** again. You'll now see a controller panel: use the **Play** button to preview your challenge and then, if you're satisfied, click the disk icon on the far right to save it.

Sharing and playing

The tour will now appear in the left sidebar. If it's in the same folder as the Placemarks, drag it out of this folder, then close the folder and uncheck the tickbox next to its name. You should also uncheck all other folders in the sidebar. This will prevent the names of the places being shown when you run the tour, which would rather give the game away. Now gather your friends and test their geographical expertise!

To email your challenge, select your tour and choose **File > Email > Email Placemark** – or you can share your tour with other Google Earth users online with **File > Share > Post**.

GOING FURTHER

Open the Google Earth Preferences for more control over how your tour will run. This brings up a dialog where you can set how long it takes to fly to each location, how long it pauses at each one, and so on.

You can also make it fly along paths, and tilt the 'camera' as it flies to view the landscape from an angle.

Google Street View: how to use it

THE GAMES

Racing with Google Maps, page 80

Street View Scavenger, page 116

Explore almost every street and road in Europe or North America – without leaving your home.

TIME 10+ mins | **DIFFICULTY ★ ★ ★** | **YOU NEED** computer with internet

Google Street View has vast and largely untapped fun potential. To get started, go to *maps.google.co.uk*.

Type in the name of the place you want to visit, or just scroll around and zoom in on anywhere that piques your curiosity, using the slider bar at the side.

The yellow figure

At the top of the zoom slider bar is a little yellow figure, who, in his eagerness to get going, starts to tilt towards you when you hover the cursor over him. Click on him and drag him over the map.

The Street View-enabled streets will highlight in blue, with a green circle or pointer showing your exact position. Pausing over a street opens a small window displaying the 'Street View' from there.

Jump in!

When you release the mouse button over a high-lit street, you'll jump into Street View and see the world from that position. There are now several things you can do:

GOING FURTHER

We have suggested a few Street View games, but we're sure there are many more possibilities. Why not invent your own Street View game, and record it in the 'Notes' section at the back of the book?

- Click and drag within the window to look around from where you're standing – or drag the 'N' around on the compass at top left
- Click on the arrows on the yellow paths to move along the road.
- Take longer 'strides' by double-clicking anywhere to go straight there (as long as the cursor brings up a rectangle or oval shape *without* a magnifying glass).
- If the cursor brings up a rectangle *with* a magnifying glass in the corner, double-click to zoom in for a closer view.

What to do next

Play some games and have some fun! (See 'The Games' on the left for some of our ideas.)

Or, if you're in a particularly practical mood, you can use Street View to:

- Scout the lie of the land before going on a journey, to make sure you don't get lost.
- Take a sneak preview of places you're thinking of going on holiday.
- Check out the parking restrictions. It's possible to zoom in close enough to read parking signs – as in the example on the right.

How to build your own website

Make a family website all by yourself, with no prior experience and at no cost.

You no longer need to spend a small fortune to produce a great-looking family website. Even with no previous experience of web design, you can create your own site and have it up and running in just a few hours.

Going the Weebly way

The easiest way to create a website is by using an online website creator. There are many options, but we found Weebly (*www.weebly.com*) especially simple to use, while still having every feature you're likely to need. We aren't alone. *Time Magazine* named it the fourth best website of 2007.

The basics

Go to *www.weebly.com*, sign up and choose your website name, which will end in 'weebly.com'. Then go to the 'design' tab and choose one of the many themes which govern the look of the website.

Pages are put together intuitively by dragging and dropping elements from the toolbar. You can have text-only sections or pictures on their own or text with pictures in them. Weebly works on a WYSIWYG (*What You See Is What You Get*) basis. Unlike some of its rivals, there are no unwanted ads to annoy visitors and cheapen the tone.

Setting up links to anything on the web takes just a click or two. The links, activated by clicking text or a picture, can even be made to email you. Just about everything you see can be customised, so you can replace the banner with your own photographs, change the layout, and so on.

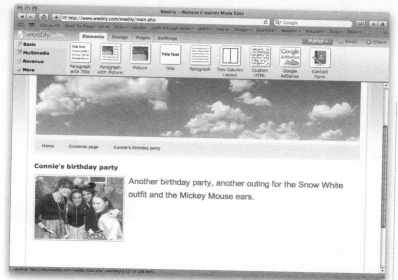

Connie's birthday party

Another birthday party, another outing for the Snow White outfit and the Mickey Mouse ears.

Beyond the basics

Give some thought to how you want the website to function. How do your favourite websites work? Your front page should link to different areas of the website, each of which may have its own set of pages. For instance, if you're creating a website for your family, the front page might have a link to a page of family news and another to a photo album. Each member of the family could have their own main page which is accessed by clicking on the front page. Blogs can also be incorporated into the design.

What do you want to do with your website?

Your website can serve as a portal for the whole family to strut their stuff. Set up a blog so every family member can record their thoughts and deeds; add art galleries to show off your creative masterpieces, or display work produced by your friends.

Do you write poems or stories? Stick them on the website so the world can read them. Or post competitions and puzzles (you'll find plenty of those in this book). And if you've uploaded your videos to YouTube, you can embed them in your Weebly site so visitors can view them directly without having to leave your page.

GOING FURTHER

Although you can be up and running with Weebly very swiftly, it is worth exploring it at leisure as it possesses many sophisticated features.

Some, such as incorporating audio and video, require you to upgrade to their 'pro' service. If you subscribe to this service you can protect your pages with passwords, have bigger file sizes, host up to 10 websites and even get your own web domain name.

Don't keep your website to yourself – let us all have a look at it.

fg-21.com/forum

How to make a 'robot eye'

THE GAMES

Eye, Robot 1,
page 20

Eye, Robot 2,
page 24

How to fix a camera phone into an old cereal box to create an amazing Robot Cereal Box Vision System™.

TIME 10 mins | **DIFFICULTY ★★★** | **YOU NEED** an old cereal box • a camera phone

Whatever the size of players' heads, you'll need the larger size of cereal boxes – at least 450g, but ideally 600g.

Cut along one narrow edge down the entire length of the box. This should give you enough room to work inside the box.

You need the phone to rest on the narrow, uncut bottom end of the box. Place the phone on the bottom of the box, lens down, and note the position of the lens. Pierce a hole in the base and expand it enough so that no cardboard will get in the way of the lens.

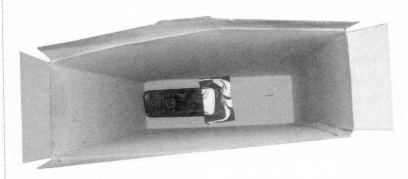

Put the phone back in position, turn on its camera and check that there is a clear view through the base of the cereal box. Once you're satisfied, fasten the mobile phone in place with tape. Then use the tape to restore the side of the box, taking special care around the opening, which needs to be tight.

Now all you need do is reach inside to switch on the camera, and place the box over your face. You're a robot!

How to make a blindfold

Several games in this book require players to be blindfolded. Here are some useful methods.

`TIME 10 mins` | `DIFFICULTY ★ ★ ★` | `YOU NEED` sleep mask, scarf, eye patches, sunglasses

Lots of our games call for a blindfold – but this isn't an item that most households have readily to hand.

These are our suggestions for good substitutes.

Sleep masks

This kind of mask is often given out on airplanes on long haul or overnight flights. Light comes in around the edges, making them less scary than proper blindfolds, without it being possible to cheat. And they're quick to remove.

Scarves

A scarf can be wrapped around a player's head, and tied with a loose knot at the back. Better, though, is to hold it at the back with a rubber band, which will be easier to take off later.

Eyepatches

Two eyepatches, either as found in pirate costume kits or as medical items bought from chemists, make excellent blindfolds – though the player does look doubly afflicted.

Sunglasses

Take a standard pair of sunglasses, and cut pieces of cardboard to cover both lenses. Fix them in place with tape. This kind of blindfold can be taken on and off very fast so is particularly useful for games where the blindfolded person has to switch often.

How to make your computer talk

THE GAMES

Robot Politician,
page 84

Both Mac and Windows computers have the ability to speak words that you type. Here's how to set them up.

TIME 15 mins | DIFFICULTY ★★★ | YOU NEED a Mac or Windows computer

Windows

Windows comes with a built-in Text to Speech system, called **Narrator**. You'll find it in **All Programs\Accessories\Accessibility**. The trouble with Narrator is that it's designed for those who have trouble seeing the screen, so it reads aloud everything the computer displays – the application name, the menus, and so on. Far too much detail for our games.

Fortunately, there's a better – and free – alternative. It's called *Ultra Hal*, named after the speaking computer in the film *2001: A Space Odyssey*. You can download it here:

fg-21.com/hal

Once downloaded, you need to install the application. When you run it, you'll see the window below. Type the text you want it to read,

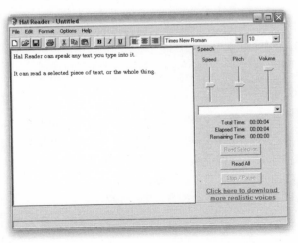

and press either the **Read Selection** or **Read All** buttons, depending on whether you want it to read just the highlighted text or the entire text typed in the editing window.

Mac OS

Every Mac comes with the **TextEdit** word processor. You can make it speak any text by choosing **Edit > Speech > Start Speaking**. However, this is a bit of a fiddle, so here's a way to speed things up by adding your own keyboard shortcut.

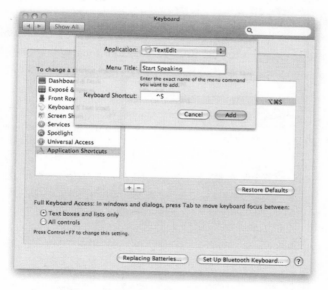

To do this, open System Preferences, and go to the Keyboard pane. Select Application Shortcuts, then click the + sign below the main pane, and choose TextEdit from the pop-up list of applications. Type 'Start Speaking' as the menu title, and choose a shortcut: we like **Ctrl S**. Click **Add** and, when you return to TextEdit, you'll be able to type **Ctrl S** to make it speak highlighted text automatically.

GOING FURTHER

With Ultra Hal, you can change the speed and pitch of the spoken voice using the on-screen sliders.

If you want to change the voice TextEdit uses, you'll need to open your Mac's System Preferences, and choose the Speech icon. This will open a list from which you can choose the voice you want, as well as the rate at which it speaks. There are some truly wacky voices there – try them out and see what you think.

How to take and crop a screen shot

THE GAMES

**Street View
Scavenger**, page
116

How to capture a portion of the screen and save it as a separate image file.

TIME 10 mins | **DIFFICULTY ★★★** | **YOU NEED** a Mac or Windows computer

It can be useful – not least for playing our Street View Scavenger game on page 116 – to crop a portion of the screen and save it as a separate file. On the Mac, it's a case of pressing a simple key combination. On Windows, the process is a little more involved. Here's how it's done.

Cropped screen shots: Windows

First, compose the view you want to capture in the frontmost window. In Google Maps or Google Street View, this will involve panning the view around within the window until it's in the right place. Here's the shot you might end up with:

If you press the **PRINT SCRN** button, you'll take a copy of the whole screen. But by holding the **alt** key at the same time, you can capture just the current window to the clipboard.

Open the **Paint** application that comes with Windows, and choose **Edit > Paste**. This will paste the screen into the Paint window. Now, use the **Marquee tool** to make a selection around the area you want – in this case, it's the clock tower:

You can now choose **Edit > Copy to...** to save just that selection to a new file. Give the file a name you'll remember, save it, and you're done.

Cropped screen shots: Mac

Press **Command Shift 3** to take a screen shot of the entire screen. Or use **Command Shift 4** intead, which will allow you to capture just a portion of the screen: simply drag to highlight the area you want, and the selection will be saved to the desktop as a .png file.

On the latest Mac OS, the file will be saved with the date and time it was captured as the file name. On earlier systems, it will be called 'Picture 0', and subsequent grabs will be labelled 'Picture 1', 'Picture 2' and so on. It's easy to rename them if you want.

EASIER CROPS

Cropping screen shots in Windows can be trickier than it needs to be. But if you have the Windows Vista Home Premium edition or later, you can use its Snipping Tool to perform a screen shot of a selected area.

For those with older versions of Windows, check out Cropper. It's a free download that will do the job in a trice. Get it here:

fg-21.com/cropper

How to upload movies to YouTube

THE GAMES

Animation for beginners, page 140

Animation: taking it further, page 142

Do-it-yourself superhero movie, page 154

Stop go: hey Presto!, page 192

Completed your cinematic masterpiece? Here's how to share it so everyone can watch.

TIME 15 mins | DIFFICULTY ★ ★ ★ | YOU NEED computer with internet

1. Sign up to YouTube

The first thing you'll need to upload your movies to You-Tube is a YouTube account. Go to *www.youtube.com* and click the **Sign Up** button to get started.

Signing up is straightfor-ward: the only difficult part is coming up with a unique user name. With millions of users all over the world, it's

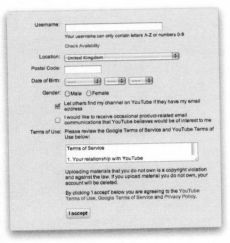

likely that your real name will already have been chosen by someone else – so get creative. You also need to enter your date of birth, nationality, gender and postcode.

2. Upload your movie

Click the **Upload** button, and you'll see this window. Click the yellow **Upload Video** button and you'll get a dialog that allows you to find your movie on your hard disk: select it and, as long as it's no longer than 10 minutes, it will start to upload.

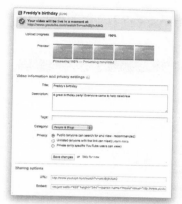

3. While it's uploading…

It can take a few minutes for a movie to upload. This is a good time to put in a title and description, and you also need to choose a category.

You can specify here if you want the movie to be public or private ('private' means either that viewers must know the URL or be invited by you).

10 MINUTES!

Standard YouTube movies can be no longer than 10 minutes – if they go over, they won't play. So if you have a long movie, you'll need to split it into shorter sections before you can upload it.

4. Edit the movie

Once the movie is uploaded, it will take a few minutes for YouTube to process it to make it viewable.

You can then edit the movie, add annotations and captions, and check it's working as it should. If you make a mistake or run into problems, you can delete the movie and start again.

5. Add a soundtrack

You can use YouTube to change your movie's soundtrack, by clicking the **AudioSwap** button. This allows you to choose from thousands of music tracks, in dozens of categories, to replace the sound in your original footage.

229

Photo trickery: how to use Pixlr

THE GAMES

Celebrity Spotter, page 10

Does my album look big in this?, page 156

Face changing photo trickery, page 160

Ghostly encounters, page 164

Pixlr (www.pixlr.com) is a powerful online image editor that costs nothing to use.

TIME 30+ mins | DIFFICULTY ★★★ | YOU NEED computer with internet

Pixlr can be used to create all kinds of fantastic effects. Here's a quick guide to how the tools and panels work.

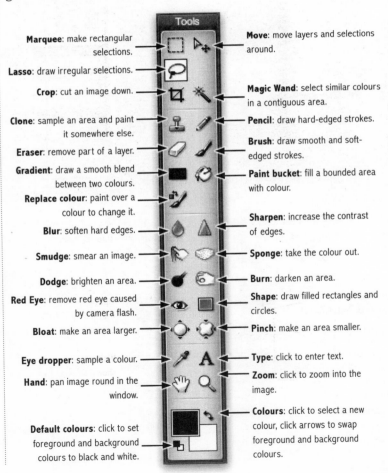

Marquee: make rectangular selections.

Lasso: draw irregular selections.

Crop: cut an image down.

Clone: sample an area and paint it somewhere else.

Eraser: remove part of a layer.

Gradient: draw a smooth blend between two colours.

Replace colour: paint over a colour to change it.

Blur: soften hard edges.

Smudge: smear an image.

Dodge: brighten an area.

Red Eye: remove red eye caused by camera flash.

Bloat: make an area larger.

Eye dropper: sample a colour.

Hand: pan image round in the window.

Default colours: click to set foreground and background colours to black and white.

Move: move layers and selections around.

Magic Wand: select similar colours in a contiguous area.

Pencil: draw hard-edged strokes.

Brush: draw smooth and soft-edged strokes.

Paint bucket: fill a bounded area with colour.

Sharpen: increase the contrast of edges.

Sponge: take the colour out.

Burn: darken an area.

Shape: draw filled rectangles and circles.

Pinch: make an area smaller.

Type: click to enter text.

Zoom: click to zoom into the image.

Colours: click to select a new colour, click arrows to swap foreground and background colours.

Menus: use the menus to save images, load selections, apply filters, and much more.

Navigator: use this to pan around an image when you're zoomed in.

Pixlr is full of special effects, filters and tools. The best way to learn it is to experiment. With the History panel, you can always undo any changes so you'll never ruin your image.

There is also plenty of help available online – to start with try www. pixlr.com/help.

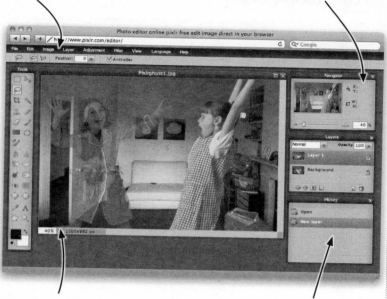

Info: shows the current zoom level, and the size of your image in pixels.

History: lists the most recent changes, and you can step back through them.

Layer mode: change the way layers interact.

Current layer: highlighted in a different colour.

Opacity: change the transparency of the current layer.

Visibility: click to hide or show a layer.

Trash: delete a layer.

New: Click to make a new layer.

Layer buttons: click to move the current layer up and down.

Mask: add a mask and paint on it to hide or show parts of a layer.

Style: add glows and other effects to a layer.

Any questions about how to use Pixlr? Ask the forum – maybe someone can help.

fg-21.com/forum

231

Reverse video

THE GAMES

Going backwards, page 166

Magical photo frames, page 174

How to make your videos play backwards.

TIME 15 mins | **DIFFICULTY ★★★** | **YOU NEED** iMovie (Mac) • FadeToBlack (Windows)

Reverse video on a Mac

Open **iMovie**. Click **Command N** to create a new Project, then choose **File > Import > Movies** and locate the clip you want to reverse. Drag the clip to the **Project** window at top left.

Double click on it then choose **Convert Entire Clip** in the **Inspector** window. This converts it to a format iMovie can work with.

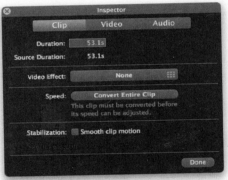

The window should now show a **Reverse** option. Select this, then click **Done**.

Test drive the result by positioning the cursor over the start of the clip in the Project window and pressing the **Space bar**. If you're satisfied use the **Share** menu at the top of the screen to export the finished movie. Otherwise, re-upload the original and try again.

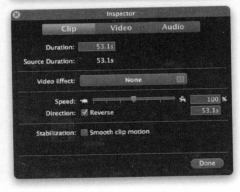

TIP: *These instructions are for iMovie 09. If you have a different version, try Googling a solution, using the above as a guide.*

Reverse video on a Windows PC

Every Windows PC comes with Windows Movie Player, but unfortunately it can't reverse video. Instead, you have to buy a separate program. We recommend **FadeToBlack**, which has a three week trial period, so you can decide if you like it before you shell out £24.95:

fg-21.com/fadetoblack

Open your movie (which must be in .avi format) and click the **Edit** button beneath the preview (1). The **Edit Clip** pane appears on the right: click **Reverse Order** (2) to set the movie to run backwards.

GOING FURTHER

FadeToBlack can only work with movies saved in .avi format. Some video cameras now save movies as .mpg or .mp4 files; you'll need to convert them to .avi files, using this free converter:

fg-21.com/avi

Found a free way to reverse video on a PC? Tell others on the forum.

fg-21.com/forum

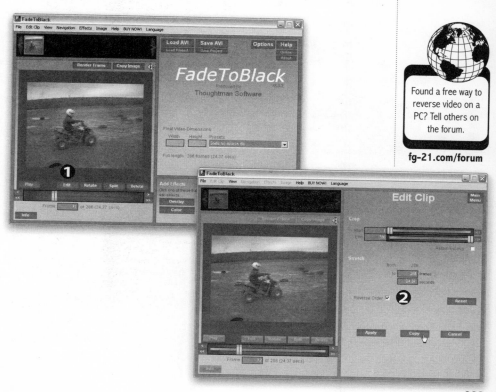

233

Stop motion movies: Mac

THE GAMES

Animation for beginners,
page 140

Animation: taking it further,
page 142

How to create your own stop motion movies – for free.

TIME 1 hour | **DIFFICULTY ★★★** | **YOU NEED** a Mac computer with iMovie installed

Not long ago you needed expensive software to make your own Aardman-style animations. Now you can do it for nothing.

Stop motion on a Mac

Once you've snapped the sequence of frames to be used in your animation, import them from your camera into the **iPhoto** application. Create a new **Event** in which to put them.

Now open **iMovie** (this is iMovie 09: other versions may vary). Press **Command N** to create and name a new Project, then choose **Window > Photos** (or press **Command 2**). Click on the **Events** icon and drag the event containing your photos into the Project window. Your soon-to-be-animated frames should now be displayed in the Project window.

Click on a still in the Project window and press **Command A** to Select All. You'll see a small cog icon as your cursor passes over any of the images.

Click on the cog, then choose **Cropping, Ken Burns and Rotation**. Three options will be shown: choose **Fit**, then click **Done**.

You now need to set iMovie to play each frame for only a fraction of a second. To do this, click on the 'cog' icon again, ensuring the frames are all still selected. This time choose **Clip Adjustments** from the menu. In the **Inspector** window, select **Clip** and change the duration to 0.1s (the minimum allowed), then check the **Applies to all stills** option, and click **Done**.

Press the **Space bar** for a trial run. If you're satisfied use the **Share** menu in the toobar to export the finished movie. If you feel a slower frame rate is needed, adjust it as before using the **Clip Adjustments** menu.

If you'd like to speed up your animation, simply re-import your footage into iMovie, drag it to a new Project window, and open the **Clip Adjustments** menu. First click **Convert Entire Clip**. A sliding scale will then appear, with a hare at one end and a tortoise at the other – use this to adjust the speed, and re-export your movie once you're happy with it.

KEN WHO?

Ken Burns is a documentary film maker who pioneered and perfected the technique of zooming and panning across still photographs to give them a sense of movement.

Apple named the technique after him when creating iMovie: it describes an automated process for bringing stills to life.

Stop motion movies: Windows

THE GAMES

Animation for beginners, page 140

Animation: taking it further, page 142

How to create your own stop motion movies – for free.

TIME 1 hour | **DIFFICULTY ★★★** | **YOU NEED** a Windows PC with JPGVideo installed

Unlike Macs, Windows computers don't have a built-in program capable of creating stop motion movies. But there's an excellent free program called **JPGVideo** that will do the job:

fg-21.com/jpgvideo

Download and install the application so it's ready for use. You'll now need to put all the photos you've taken for the project into a separate folder, if you haven't done this already.

Open the **JPGVideo** application. You'll be prompted for the **JPG Directory** (1) – this is the location of the folder containing all the images from the camera. You'll also need to specify the **Output** (2), which is where you want to save the movie. Set the **Frames per second** to around 8 (3), and click **OK** (4).

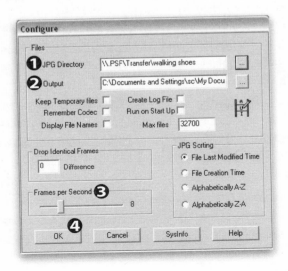

A new dialog will pop up, which allows you to build your movie from the images you've selected: click **Run** (5).

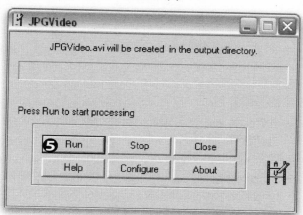

Another dialog will appear, asking you to select a Codec. This is a method of compressing the video to a smaller size. If you don't mind the movies taking up a lot of space, leave the codec as **Full Frame (Uncompressed)**; for a smaller file size, choose **Cinepak** (6) and then click **OK** (7). Your movie will be created in the directory you specified. JPGVideo can't play the movie, but you can open it in **Windows Media Player** to see how it has turned out.

Brain power, tricks and puzzle games

Creative games

Active games

Party games

Indoor games

Outdoor games

Car games

Your notes

Your notes

Your notes

Your notes

Join us online

Technology is advancing so fast that, even a few years ago, many of the games and activities in this book couldn't have existed. There must be plenty of other creative ways of using gadgets that we haven't thought of.

We'd love it if you shared your ideas and experiences on our website. There's a Reader Forum for you to suggest new games or ways of refining existing ones. Feel free to blow your own trumpet if you've created something you're particularly proud of.

We'll use the site ourselves to post updates, new game ideas, and other fun stuff we come across.

Come and join the Fun and Games Revolution:

www.fg-21.com